newrooms

A practical home makeover guide

Sally and Stewart Walton

p

This is a Parragon Book

First published in 2001

Parragon

Queen Street House

4 Queen Street

Bath BA1 1HE, UK

Created and produced for Parragon by The Bridgewater Book Company Ltd.

Creative Director Stephen Knowlden

Art Director Michael Whitehead

Editorial Director Fiona Biggs

Project Editor Sarah Bragginton

Designer Alistair Plumb

Photography Alistair Hughes

Picture Research Lynda Marshall

Illustrations Stewart Walton

ISBN: 0-75256-482-X (Hardback)
ISBN: 0-75256-734-9 (Paperback)

Printed in China

newrooms

Contents

Introduction   6

Kitchens   8

Country/Contemporary/1950s/Galley

Sitting Rooms   42

Traditional/Contemporary/Global/Tiny

Dining Rooms   76

Traditional/Contemporary/Sitting-Dining

Bedrooms   98

Traditional/Contemporary/Teenage Boy's/Teenage Girl's/

Children's/Fantasy/Nursery

Bathrooms   154

Traditional/Contemporary/Shower Room

Fun & Study   184

Office-Living Space/Home Office/Teenager's Study/Child's Playroom

Colour & Light   224

Using Colour to Create Moods/Using Lighting Effectively

Accessories   236

Mini Projects   240

Lampshades/Cushions/Frames

Suppliers   248

Index   254

Acknowledgements   256

Introduction

A 1950s breakfast bar is just one of the many inexpensive projects you can do by following the step-by-step instructions in this book.

You don't need to go out and buy new furniture to give a room a new look. A new throw like this one on an elderly sofa can introduce strong colour contrasts and a more relaxed style, as well as covering marks on old upholstery.

In the past, decorating was seen as a necessary chore, but these days it has become one of the most popular leisure activities. The aim of this book is to make decorating your home simple, inexpensive and more fun than ever before. We live in the age of the make-over, and there has never been more choice available to the home decorator than there is now. There are more materials, books, television programmes and magazines about decorating and interior design that there have ever been before, and the only downside is that there is often too much choice when it comes to deciding what you want! It is easy to make a decision about a colour if there are only ten to choose from, but if you are faced with 200 subtle variations of blue, it's enough to confuse even the most experienced decorator.

The best way to stay sane and enjoy the decorating process is to have a clear idea of what you want and what you are going to do before you hit the shops. This means taking time to decide on colour, style and content by watching the television programmes, looking in magazines and stores, then finding out how to get the look you're after by following the well-designed and inspirational step-by-step projects in this book.

New Rooms takes you through the entire home, offering a choice of traditional or contemporary ideas for each room. Many of the ideas will easily translate into other decorative styles, and can be adapted for use in other parts of the house. As many techniques are covered as possible; for example the various flooring options that are available have been allocated to certain rooms, but the process of painting a wooden floor will be the same, whether donc in a kitchen or a bathroom. You may well find that the ideal storage solution for your kitchen is one that is suggested in the nursery section, so be sure to have a look at all the projects before making up your mind.

The step-by-steps have been kept as clear and concise as possible – it is usually the case that too many instructions are as confusing as too few. As most DIY products come complete with their own set of instructions, these have been taken as read in many cases and the step-by-steps just show how to put the actual idea into practice. The most vital product and tool instructions and advice to follow are those that relate to your safety. The statistics for DIY accidents in the home show that many could have been avoided if only

the safety advice on many of these tools had been followed.

So, if you plan to do up a whole house, decorate a room from scratch or just make stylish improvements, we hope this book gives you with all the inspiration and information that you need.

Practical storage solutions like this disguised drawer on castors can be adapted for different rooms in the house, from the office to children's bedrooms.

Kitchens

The kitchen is often regarded as the heart of the home. It is the room where meals are prepared and is often a place to eat, gather and socialise, so function plays a large part in the style. This section shows you how to transform your kitchen into three different styles: Country, Contemporary and 1950s. Every kitchen can achieve these styles, whatever its size or shape, but an additional section shows you how to make the most of a galley kitchen. The three step-by-step projects will start you off, and a few accessories and a fresh coat of paint will do the rest. Have fun!

Country kitchen

For most of us, country living is a bit of a daydream, and if there is one aspect we would like more than anything it is the traditional country kitchen. The idea of sitting at a large, scrubbed pine table, with the smell of baking and jars of home-made pickles and jam on the shelves is very appealing, especially when your own kitchen has fitted melamine with all the charm of a school canteen! Don't despair though; that country kitchen of your dreams may not be possible, but there is a lot that can be done to inject any kitchen with all the key ingredients.

Begin by listing the top 10 features that say 'country' to you, loud and clear. They might go something like this…

1 Gingham

2 Baskets

3 Pine table and chairs

4 Old-fashioned sink with brass taps

5 A wooden dish drainer

6 Curtains instead of blinds

7 Open shelves or a dresser

8 Solid fuel cooker

9 Busy walls with a display of plates

10 Quarry tiled floor

Realistically, your existing kitchen may be too small for a table and chairs, the floor may not be strong enough to support a solid fuel cooker, and you may have to make do with your stainless steel sink and the vinyl floor, but this doesn't mean that you can't go country in other ways. There are loads of things you can do to make a practical modern kitchen feel more homely.

Natural colours

Start with the colour, and if it is bright white and shiny it can be mellowed with a soft yellow wash, while if it is too boring and beige it can be spiced up with rusty red. Country colours are never harsh and tend to echo nature and the countryside. Stencilled patterns make a very good background to the busy look that is so typically country. And more is definitely better when it comes to hanging pictures, plates and kitchen utensils on the walls.

Soft lighting

Lighting can also make a real difference. You certainly need to see what you're doing and there is no denying that spotlights are useful, but they are also real atmosphere killers. A simple wrought-iron candelabra or a frosted-glass shade hung low over the table will create a more relaxed feeling, especially when fitted with a dimmer switch to vary the brilliance.

On display

A key aspect of the country look is having lots on show. You may not own a large Welsh dresser loaded with crockery, but a couple of wide plank shelves above a base unit can soon be dressed up to look like one. Simply paint the wall, shelves and cupboard below the same colour, add rows of cup hooks below the shelves and brass drawer handles, and then make a display of your kitchen crockery.

You can buy rolls of self-adhesive vinyl in gingham checks, using it to line drawers and shelves. Invest in a good quality, checked PVC

A pine table and chairs, a solid fuel cooker and open shelves of crockery are features of a typical country kitchen, but there are other ways you can adopt the country style and give your kitchen a more homely feel.

tablecloth, and look around for odd wooden chairs in junk shops, and then paint them all the same colour to make a non-matching set.

Distressed paintwork

Distressed paintwork is still one of the key features in the country style because it gives the impression of having both a family history and a relaxed attitude. Fake it by applying contrasting coloured paint in two coats, and sanding away the top coat in places to simulate wear and tear. Use matt paint and finish it off with a topcoat of beeswax polish, which looks and smells heavenly.

Country kitchens should also feel cosy in the evenings, so ditch the blinds and choose curtains

instead. Shaker-style patterned fabric featuring ticking stripes, tiny checks or plaid patterns will all look good in the kitchen, and if you have a sewing machine, a simple plain border and some hand-stitched button detailing will add a contemporary touch. Some matching curtain ties in the same fabric will complete the look.

THE PROJECTS

The three projects on the following pages will help you achieve a country-style background in your own kitchen. A few carefully selected accessories, a fresh coat of paint and some warm, relaxed lighting will do the rest.

More is better than less in a country-style kitchen, so have as much as possible on display. Cover wall space with shelves of crockery, cups on hooks and small wooden cupboards, and replace modern drawer handles with brass versions.

YOU WILL NEED:
- 9-MM MDF
- FINE-GRADE SANDPAPER
- FACE MASK
- JIGSAW
- 8-MM DRILL BIT
- ALL-SURFACE PRIMER
- PAINT (SATIN OR EGGSHELL FINISH)
- GLOSS ROLLER AND SMALL ROLLER TRAY
- 12-MM CHICKEN WIRE (OR NEAREST GAUGE TO THIS)
- WIRE CUTTERS
- SMALL HAMMER
- STAPLE GUN

PROJECT ONE

Replacing existing doors with chicken wire, framed in MDF

This project is suitable for wall-mounted kitchen or base units. If you like the look you could use it throughout the kitchen, but remember that you can see through chicken wire and not everything in a cupboard makes a good display.

Begin by emptying the cupboard and unscrewing the door. Kitchen cupboard hinges tend to leave large holes which will need filling if you are changing the style. Clean the inside of the cupboard with a grease-cutting detergent and paint it a country colour – pale moss green or slate blue, for instance. Melamine will need to be primed first, ideally with an all-surface primer. If you are lining the shelves, do it at this stage before the door is replaced.

Replacing existing cupboard doors with chicken wire suits the country-kitchen look because it puts more of your kitchen on show. It's a good idea to plan the contents of the cupboards before you put them on display.

HOW TO DO IT

STEP 1 Place your outgoing door on top of the MDF. Use it as as a template, drawing the outline onto the MDF. Clamp the MDF on a workbench and wear the mask as you cut it to size, and sand the edges lightly.

STEP 2 Draw the cut-out shape onto the MDF. Drill a hole in one corner of the shape, using an 8-mm drill bit.

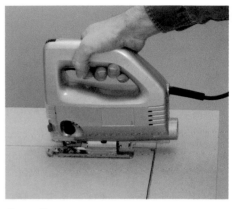

STEP 3 Clamp the MDF to the workbench and jigsaw out the inside shape. Keep the jigsaw's foot in touch with the surface of the MDF, and move with the saw.

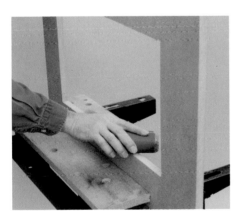

STEP 4 Use sandpaper to smooth the edge on the inside and outside. Always wear a mask when sanding MDF to prevent you breathing in the fine particles which contain chemicals best avoided!

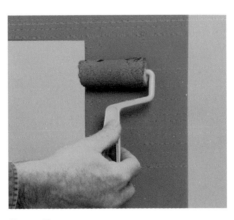

STEP 5 Give the door two coats of primer, following the drying times as directed on the can. Use a foam roller to apply the paint because it will give a better finish than a brush, and painting takes half the time. Apply the top coat in the same way.

STEP 6 Cut the chicken wire to the size of the cut-out shape allowing an extra 25 mm all around the edge. Turn over a seam of 10 mm and flatten it with a hammer. Lay the MDF face down with the chicken wire in position at the back. Staple the panel at the four cardinal points first, then add more staples in between until it is perfectly secure. Re-hang the door.

TIP
• Chicken wire, even with a folded seam, has sharp pointy edges. As long as the shelves in the cupboard are set back from the door, it is a good idea to cover up these edges with a simple wooden moulding.
• Measure the lengths required, then mitre the corners and use panel pins to secure them.

YOU WILL NEED:
- SCREWDRIVER
- WOOD FILLER
- MOULDING
- MITRING SAW (OR
  TENON SAW AND
  MITRING BLOCK)
- MEDIUM-GRADE
  SANDPAPER
- CONTACT ADHESIVE
- MOULDING PINS
- SMALL HAMMER
- ALL-PURPOSE PRIMER
- PAINT (IN A SUITABLE
  COUNTRY COLOUR)
- SMALL FOAM PAINT
  ROLLER AND TRAY
- WILLOW BASKETS

PROJECT TWO

Removing cupboard doors and adding willow baskets

Any base unit or kitchen cupboard can be given a real country look by removing the doors, and using willow baskets on the shelves as pull-out drawers. In fact, it may require a leap of the imagination to convert a standard beige melamine cupboard into something beautiful, but it can be done! All you need do is whip off the doors, fill the holes and pop in the baskets, but a few trimmings will make all the difference.

A melamine cupboard can be painted after suitable priming, and the facing edges of the cupboard can be covered with a wooden moulding. They come in a range of styles, from twisted rope and oak leaves to simple half-moon and square edge. The inside of the cupboard will look good painted in a contrasting colour to the outside, and there is also the option of adding a curtain on a simple net wire. Checked gingham or even linen tea towel curtains look a million times better than old melamine, and they can be tied back to reveal the baskets inside.

Willow baskets as sliding, pull-out shelves transforms standard melamine cupboards. Paint the insides and outsides of the cupboard first, and add wooden moulding to the facing edges.

HOW TO DO IT

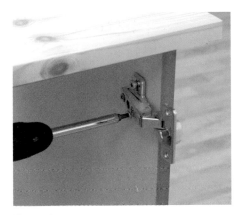

STEP 1 Unscrew the existing doors and remove the fittings. Fill the holes with wood filler so that the filler stands slightly proud of the surface. Once it has dried, sand the filler level.

STEP 2 Measure the frame then cut the moulding to fit, mitring the corners. Apply contact adhesive to the frame.

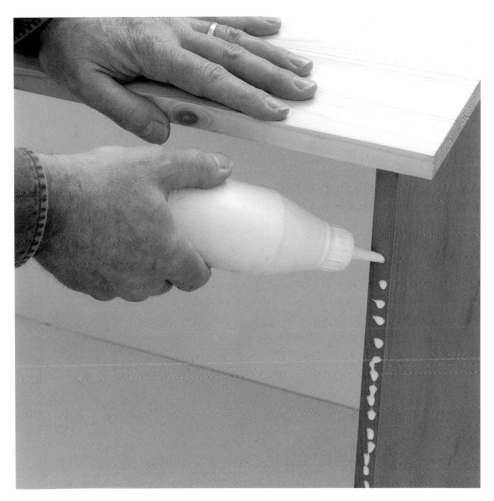

STEP 3 Stick the moulding down and then add a few pins along each length. Tap the pinheads into the moulding with a nail punch, fill the holes and sand smooth.

STEP 4 Prime the cupboard and then paint it inside and out. If you are using two different colours, paint the inside of the cupboard first and allow it to dry before painting the area where the colours meet.

BASKET HANDLE IDEAS
You can use any of the following...
• Cardboard parcel labels tied on with string
• Checked ribbons
• Stitched tubes of fabric
• Threaded beads or buttons on twists of wire
• Rope loops
• Buckled leather straps

STEP 5 Buy willow baskets to fill the space widthways, leaving just enough room for them to slide easily in and out. Many baskets have handles attached, but if not there are plenty of ways to make your own.

YOU WILL NEED:

- HOCKEY-STICK
  MOULDING (MEASURE
  THE DEPTH OF THE
  WORKTOP AND ADD
  TO IT THE DEPTH OF
  THE TILE PLUS 1 CM OF
  ADHESIVE FOR THE
  MOULDING HEIGHT,
  AND ALL AROUND THE
  EDGE OF THE
  WORKTOP FOR THE
  LENGTH)
- CONTACT ADHESIVE
- FINE PINS
- NAIL PUNCH
- SMALL HAMMER
- MITRING SAW (OR
  TENON SAW AND
  MITRING BLOCK)
- WOOD FILLER
- TILES
- TILE ADHESIVE
- GROUT
- SPONGE

PROJECT THREE

Tiling a worktop

One thing you won't find in a perfect country kitchen is a vinyl laminated worktop. Wood or tiles are the look to go for, but the wood has to be well seasoned and solid, which is very pricey. Tiles are the better option, and laying them on a flat surface is not only easy but fun. They will give you the country look for next to nothing and have maximum make-over power. The worktop is edged with a hockey-stick moulding which has a flat edge and a rounded top resting on top of the tile, giving a very neat, professional finish.

Choose traditional-style, plain deep greens or blues, or cream for the dairy look. Quarry tiles are another option but grease will mark them, so keep them away from the cooking area. A cheap and cheerful idea is to buy a range of different-coloured tiles that are all the same size. End-of-line tiles are often sold off cheaply and can be laid to look like a patchwork quilt pattern. Most importantly, measure the area that needs tiling carefully and buy the correct number of tiles to fit the space.

Tiles are one of the easiest and cheapest ways of giving your worktops a country-kitchen make-over. Edge them with a hockey-stick moulding to give a neat, professional finish.

HOW TO DO IT

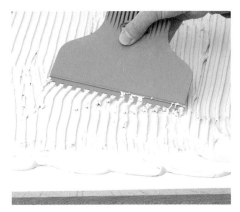

STEP 1 Have a trial run by laying out the tiles to get an idea of their spacing. Ideally you will have bought tiles which fit snugly to the edges of the worktop. If you do need to do any cutting, borrow a good tile cutter because it will make the job so much easier.

STEP 2 Spread ceramic tile adhesive over the surface to an even depth of about 1 cm. Comb the surface of the adhesive into ridges with a spreading tool.

STEP 3 Press the tiles into the bed of the adhesive, beginning at the front corner, working along the front and then filling in the rows behind. Aim to leave an equal gap between the tiles. Wipe off any adhesive which squeezes out while it is still wet, and then leave to set.

STEP 6 Apply contact adhesive to the front edge of the worktop. Rest the top of the moulding on the tiles, and flatten it down onto the adhesive at the front. Fit two sides the same way, then tap in a few fine pins to help secure them and punch their heads below the surface with a nail punch. Fill the small holes, and then paint or varnish the moulding.

STEP 4 Apply a generous amount of the grouting mixture, working it into the gaps between the tiles. Wipe off most of the excess with a damp sponge and leave to set. Wipe again when it is semi-dry.

STEP 5 Measure the lengths of moulding you need, and cut the adjoining pieces to a 45° angle with a mitring saw. Only the front corners need mitring if the worktop is to stand against the wall.

Contemporary kitchen

The contemporary kitchen is a fusion between professional catering style and the comforts of home. This is the antidote to clutter and the minimalist's idea of heaven. It may seem impossible to maintain this chic modern look, keeping worktops free of clutter, but with well-planned storage space and a little daily discipline, it can be easier than you think to achieve the contemporary style.

The best tables in a contemporary kitchen are simple fold-aways or small, round café-style versions, which do not interfere with the clean lines.

At its most extreme the look is cold and industrial with steel, concrete, glass and large no-frills appliances that mimic a restaurant kitchen. The irony is that it is a style favoured by wealthy urban loft dwellers who eat out most of the time! However, in the same way that haute couture inspires the high street fashion, the extreme version of industrial chic is the inspiration for a more practical, comfortable and achievable home style. The top 10 elements to go for are…

Stainless steel appliances

They echo the catering style but are scaled down to a more realistic size, while worktops are granite or marble, or resin compounds which look the part but are not as heavy or expensive as the real thing. Accessorise with stainless steel handles, utensils, light fittings and sink units. Small details like stainless steel sockets and shelf supports will also make a big impact.

Stainless steel appliances and granite or marble worktops bring the professional catering style into the home. Stainless steel handles, utensils, light fittings and sink units add to the impact.

Pale wooden units

Plain, pale wood like beech or ash provides a perfect complement to steel, and this is where the homely look breaks ranks with industrial chic, because wood is warm and organic. Keep the doors plain with steel handles, and avoid drawers above cupboards if you can. A set of drawers on their own are actually more practical, and the look is more contemporary.

Floating wooden strip floor

This is laid on top of the existing floor – what could be simpler? All that's needed is a dry, level surface, a polystyrene sheet underlay and enough laminated floorboards to fit the room. The boards come in a range of wood finishes and the quality will be reflected in the price, which, with luck, includes a free fitting.

Frosted glass shelves

Frosted glass is cool. Use the reinforced version for shelves, supported by stainless steel brackets, as panels in doors, or design and make your own frosted window with masking tape, templates and etching spray.

Limited colour range

When it comes to choosing colour, think pale and interesting. Bright white is too stark and reflective, but pale grey, off-white, duck-egg blue or light sea green all suit this look. For a subtle toned effect pick a colour and its immediate neighbours on the chart. Try and avoid strong contrasts and go for harmonies instead.

Slatted blinds

Blinds provide the neatest window treatment but only if they fit perfectly and work efficiently. Roller blinds are neat and good value, but the ideal blind for this look is the slatted Venetian blind. Aluminium or light wood both look fabulous, and you can adjust them in several ways to filter the incoming light.

No clutter on worktops

The no clutter rule has to be strictly enforced if this look is to succeed! Real life is not a clutter-free zone and the only way to achieve this is by being very organised, with good storage and a place for everything. Lighten the look with fresh flowers or a row of herbs in matching pots.

Chrome rails with matching utensils

Utensils don't belong in drawers, but they do need to be visible and well within reach. The best way to arrange them is by hanging them on a fitted rail above the worktop. This type of rail with hooks can be bought in a range of lengths and styles, or follow the simple instructions in the project and make your own.

Contemporary kitchen table and matching set of chairs or stools

The table is not the main attraction in a contemporary kitchen. A small, round café-style table or a simple fold-away version is a good idea, especially in small spaces, and avoid cluttering the no-frills look. Chairs are now very much in fashion, and there are so many new designs to choose from. Whether you go for lightweight, cast aluminium chairs, smooth beech with

chrome legs, or folding metal and polypropylene in jelly colours, it is hard to go wrong.

Recessed downlights in ceiling, or halogen spotlights

To see what you're doing in the kitchen, a combination of good task lighting and an ambient glow is ideal. Recessed ceiling lights look great but there are restrictions on their use. Better still, use strip lights fitted below the wall cupboards or you could opt for a row of halogen spotlights angled to illuminate the work area.

Worktops are kept clutter free in a contemporary kitchen, so good storage space and planning a place for everything is a must.

THE PROJECTS

The three projects on the following pages will help you achieve a contemporary background in your own kitchen. A few stainless steel accessories, a fresh coat of paint and some halogen lighting will do the rest.

PROJECT ONE

Replacing existing doors

A change of doors on the kitchen units is one of the quickest ways to create a new look. Fitted kitchen units are made to a standard size and, although the hinges look quite complex, they are not difficult to fit. Ready-made hardwood doors are widely available and it makes sense to use them if the style is right. The other option is to make them yourself using beech-faced MDF. You get the best of both worlds with a material like this. The MDF backing makes it easy to work with, and the beech facing has all the beauty of the natural grain. You can buy it from most good timber merchants in sheets measuring 12 m x 2.4 m in a standard 19 mm thickness.

Replacing kitchen unit doors is one of the quickest ways to create a new look. Since fitted kitchen units are made to a standard size, you can buy them ready made. Add chrome handles to complete the look.

HOW TO DO IT

STEP 1 Support the door as you unscrew the hinges to remove it. If the screws are in a good condition, save them to re-use in the new door.

STEP 2 If you are making a new door then use the old one as a template to draw around. Check the right-angles and the measurements, and then cut out the new door with a handsaw and sandpaper the edges.

STEP 3 Mark the positions for the hinge fittings, and drill out the recess with the spade bit.

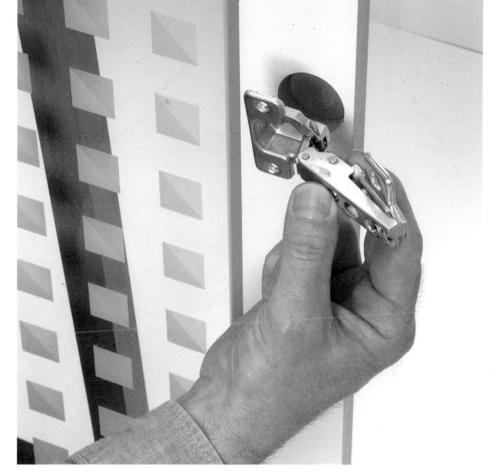

STEP 4 Hold the door in position with the hinge mechanism fitted into the recess, and mark the screw positions. Drill small pilot holes.

STEP 5 Screw the hinges to the doors. The fit of the door can be adjusted using the two screws on the hinge inside the cupboard. Loosen the screws, move the door slightly and re-tighten them. Repeat this sequence until the fit is perfect.

STEP 6 Measure the positions for the screws or bolts accurately. The handles on all the doors must be perfectly aligned, so double check and use a spirit level. Drill holes for the screws or bolts and fit the handles.

YOU WILL NEED:
- STEEL OR CHROME RAIL WITH HOOKS (OR TWO CHROME TOWEL RAIL HOLDERS AND A LENGTH OF RAIL)
- STRAIGHT EDGE WITH A BUILT-IN SPIRIT LEVEL
- MASKING TAPE IF THE WALL IS TILED
- DRILL
- CORRECT SIZE MASONRY DRILL BIT FOR THE SCREWS (EG SCREW SIZE No. 6, BIT SIZE No. 6)
- WALL PLUGS FOR A BRICK WALL (OR CAVITY WALL PLUGS FOR STUD WALLS)

PROJECT TWO

Fitting a chrome utensil rail to the wall

The first thing you need to discover is what your wall is made of. The usual suspects are painted or tiled brick or plasterboard, and they require different wall fixings. There is also a knack to drilling holes in tiles successfully. Use a small strip of masking tape which has to be placed on the tile before you mark the screw position. The tape stops the drill bit from skidding off as it spins. Whether you buy a ready-made rail or make one yourself by customising a chrome towel rail, the actual task of fitting it to the wall will be the same.

Chrome utensil rails can be bought ready-made or you can make them by customising a chrome towel rail. When you are deciding which height to fit it, hang the longest utensil from the rail to make sure it's high enough.

HOW TO DO IT

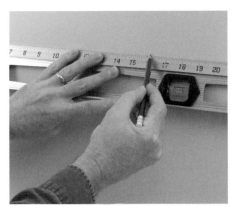

STEP 1 Decide where you would like the rail on the wall. Do this with the longest of the utensils hanging from it. Place strips of masking tape on the tiles roughly where holes need to be drilled.

STEP 2 Hold up the rail to the wall with the spirit level. Make certain that the rail is level, then accurately mark the positions for the screws. Drill the holes for the wall plugs. Hold the drill at a right angle to the wall and apply firm pressure as you drill.

TIPS
• Chrome rails can be clamped to a workbench or a table edge, and cut down to size with a hacksaw.
• Wooden dowelling rods can be used with chrome towel rail fittings to give a softer look. They are especially suitable if you have wooden floors or cupboard doors.
• Buy butcher-style hooks, without sharp points, from kitchenware shops.

STEP 3 Push the plugs into the holes, tapping them lightly with a hammer if necessary. They should fit snugly and stay in place. If the hole is too big you may need to go up a size with both wall plugs and screws.

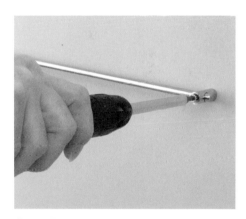

STEP 4 Screw in the top screw on each side to support the rail as you tighten the other screws.

YOU WILL NEED:
• SCREWDRIVER
• WOOD FILLER
• SANDPAPER
• SET OF NEW HANDLES
• SPIRIT LEVEL
• DRILL FITTED WITH
  A BIT TO MATCH THE
  BOLT SIZE

PROJECT THREE

Changing handles

This is an easy project to provide an instant lift. Fashions change, thank goodness, and at the moment knobs are out and long thin steel handles are in. They are usually fixed with bolts which screw in from the back of the door. It is a style which only suits plain doors and drawers because the look emphasises clean lines and good design. If you have doors with mouldings and panels then consider replacing the doors altogether, or facing them with hardboard or 6-mm MDF stuck down with panel adhesive.

Fitting new handles on kitchen units provides an instant lift. Long, thin steel handles emphasise clean lines, so they only suit plain doors.

HOW TO DO IT

STEP 1 Unscrew the old handles or knobs and fill the holes. When the filler has dried, sand it flat and touch up the paint or varnish. You may decide to take this opportunity to refresh all the paintwork, but that is another story.

STEP 2 Decide on the position for the new handle which can be fitted horizontally or vertically about 25 mm from the door edge – both ways look good. Check it with the spirit level then mark the fitting positions.

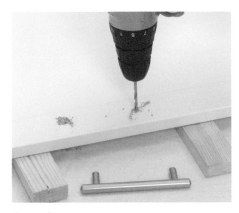

STEP 3 Drill the holes for the bolts. Check each hole against the next mark with the spirit level before you drill the hole.

STEP 4 Tighten the screws or bolts from the back of the door; you can hold the handles if it makes it easier.

TIPS
• If you are changing the handles on a row of units, it is vital to fit them in a straight line. Make a cardboard template with the bolt positions drilled out. This can be placed against the back of each cupboard to make sure that the handle positions do not vary.

The 1950s kitchen
Sometimes it seems that colour was invented in the 1950s because everything before that was photographed in black and white. In truth, homes were pretty dull during the war years, but it was also a time of great advances in technology and design. When all the brainpower and new materials were no longer needed for the war effort, thoughts turned towards the commercial world.

Formica worktops are a key element in any 1950s-style kitchen, along with contrasting colours such as primrose yellow used with black. Streamlined, rocket-shaped bins and other appliances complete the look.

The 1950s kitchen is a part of the American dream, fitted with bright Formica worktops, shiny chrome appliances, colourful plastics and checked lino flooring. It started in America but the look took off across the Atlantic as soon as it was seen in those Doris Day movies. Keep an eye out for 1950s cookery books in charity shops or second-hand book shops because they offer a wealth of inspiration. Genuine 1950s kitchen units are collectors' items now, but you can still pick up kitchen accessories in junk shops and specialist stores. The 1950s revival is always simmering away on the back burner and kitchen furniture with that look features in many contemporary ranges, mixing chrome, leather, Formica and fun. The top 10 ingredients that make the 1950s style kitchen are…

Rounded, streamlined steel and chrome appliances

The streamlined style was inspired by the advent of the jet plane and excitement surrounding space rocket missions. Sleek chrome striping was used to make stationary kitchen appliances look as though they were speeding! Everything from fridges to food mixers were given this look, and some of the best designs are still in production today. Look out for reconditioned fridges and repro toasters, chrome bins, kettles, blenders, kitchen clocks and radios. Since they are still a popular style, they shouldn't be hard to find.

Red and white chequerboard vinyl floor

Some of the least expensive floor tiles on the market are slightly marble-ised, self-adhesive, plain-coloured vinyl. They have the look of authentic 1950s lino but at a fraction of the cost. Go for a big colour contrast – red and white or yellow and black chequerboard floors may not appeal to the faint-hearted, but when you see them reflected in the chromework – wow!

Small black-and-white chequered borders

Small, black-and-white chequered borders seen on the sides of New York taxicabs often feature in 1950s-style diners. There are two ways to get the same effect without re-tiling the kitchen: one is to apply the chequerboard pattern on a self-adhesive tape strip, and the other is to print the border with a rubber roller stamp, bought from a specialist crafts' supplier.

Walls painted in contrasting colours

Colour in the 1950s was all about contrasts. Pale colours like eau de nil (a light green) or primrose yellow and sky blue were often used with black. And you can't fail with red, whether it's just the plastic handles of cupboards and drawers or a whole wall painted in red gloss. Different-coloured walls, or blocks of strong colour on a part of a pale wall are the look to go for.

Patterns – polka dots and stars

One of the most popular patterns for wallpaper in the 1950s had small white stars or spots on a coloured background which would be used on just one wall. Tablecloths and curtains were made from polka-dot fabric reversed out, where the pattern colour swapped over with the background colour.

Formica

Formica is the plastic laminate that revolutionised kitchen worktops. It is one of the key elements in any 1950s-style kitchen. Choose bright yellow, cherry red or sky blue for a big impact, and take it up the wall behind the worktop as a splashback.

Tubular steel

If you ever see a set of old chrome steel kitchen chairs then buy them, regardless of the state of the upholstery. Re-cover the seats with soft vinyl stapled in place, edged with a row of chrome upholstery studs. These retro-style kitchen tables and chairs are back in fashion and are really pricey, so cheat if you possibly can.

Kitsch

Kitsch is the German word for bad taste, but sometimes bad taste is actually good taste, especially when it is entirely deliberate! Think of Elvis in *Blue Hawaii* with plastic fruit and flowers, sunsets, neon signs, flying ducks, laminated calenders and anything plastic in the shape of a poodle!

THE PROJECTS

The three projects on the following pages will help you achieve a 1950s background in your own kitchen. A few kitsch accessories, some streamlined chrome appliances and some black-and-white checkered borders will do the rest.

Colourful modern ceramics

Organic shapes, Picasso-inspired patterns and bright contrasting colours give 1950s ceramics a highly distinctive look. These things are within everyone's budget, so get out there and start looking. Try inexpensive car boot sales and junk shops but if you can't spare the time to trawl, find a market trader who specialises in 1950s ware.

Packaging and plastics

Quite a lot of cheap plastic ware manufactured in the Far East fits in well with this look. American mustard in a bright yellow squeezy bottle or a large plastic tomato filled with ketchup helps to set the scene. You do have to be selective, but that is the fun of putting a themed look together.

Chequerboard vinyl floors can be bought as self-adhesive tiles at a fraction of the cost of authentic 1950s lino. The bigger the contrast in colours the better.

YOU WILL NEED:

- WET AND DRY
  SANDPAPER
- ALL-SURFACE PRIMER
- SMALL FOAM ROLLER
  WITH TRAY
- METHYLATED SPIRIT
  (FOR CLEANING)
- SATINWOOD PAINT
  IN PALE GREEN
  (MAIN COLOUR)
- STENCIL MATERIAL
  (CARD OR PLASTIC)
- CRAFT KNIFE
- TRACING PAPER
  (OR PHOTOCOPIES
  OF PATTERNS)
- MATCH POT OF BRIGHT
  RED (BACKGROUND
  COLOUR)
- MATCH POT OF BLACK
  (FOR THE PATTERN)

PROJECT ONE

Painting the kitchen units

The idea that melamine kitchen units can be painted is actually quite new. This has a lot to do with TV make-over programmes and the popularity of home style magazines. Once the make-over idea took off people started experimenting, trying different products and discovering new uses for old materials.

The problem with a shiny surface like melamine is that, without the right primer, the paint has nothing to key into and is easily scratched. The trick is to scratch the surface with a wet and dry sandpaper, then apply one or two coats of a shellac-based primer. It gives good coverage, is very strong and leaves an ultra-matt surface.

Go creative on your kitchen units! Melamine kitchen units can be painted as long as they are prepared beforehand, using sandpaper to scratch the surface and primer to give an ultra-matt surface.

HOW TO DO IT

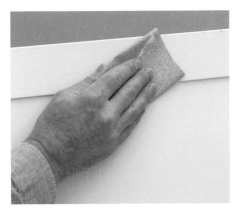

STEP 1 Clean the doors with a grease-cutting detergent or sugar soap. Rub them down with wet and dry sandpaper to remove the shine from the surface.

STEP 2 Apply the primer with the roller and leave to dry (repeat if necessary). Apply the main colour (repeat if necessary).

STEP 3 Enlarge the two stencil patterns and transfer them onto a stencil card or plastic. Cut them out with a craft knife. Paint the background shapes first in the light colour.

STEP 4 Use the second stencil to apply the pattern inside the shapes, and then apply two coats of clear gloss varnish.

Enlarge the stencils and transfer them onto plastic or stencil paper. The guides to the left will help you position the two main stencils together on your kitchen unit door.

YOU WILL NEED:
- TAPE MEASURE
- SHEET METAL
- DOMED CAPPED
  MIRROR SCREWS
- DRILL
- MASONRY BIT TO
  MATCH SCREW SIZE
- WALL PLUGS TO
  MATCH SCREW SIZE

PROJECT TWO

Fitting a stainless steel, zinc or aluminium splashback

Measure the size of the splashback area then visit a sheet metal dealer. They cut metal sheets to size and will usually have a stock of off-cuts suitable for small jobs like this. Explain what you will be using it for, and check that the type you have chosen will keep its shine and never rust. They have the right equipment, so ask for the sheet to be cut to size and for the edges to be buffed. There may be a charge for this service but it will be worth it!

Metal sheets can be bought as off-cuts from a sheet metal dealer and cut to size with the edges buffed. You can drill holes in the sheet using the same bit as you use for wood.

HOW TO DO IT

STEP 1 Measure the splashback area. Don't have it too narrow because it needs to be about one third of the depth of the worktop. Mark the positions of the screws with a nail punch.

STEP 2 Holes can be drilled in sheet metal using the same bit as you use for wood. You will need to have a wall fixing approximately every 25 cm on a long strip. Drill all the screw holes in the metal, and then hold it in position as you mark the screw positions on the wall.

STEP 3 Drill the screw holes in the wall then push in the wall plugs. If you are fitting this on a solid wall use regular wall plugs, but for a stud wall you need cavity wall plugs which grip from the back.

STEP 4 Place the splashback against the wall and screw it in place. Screw the domed caps into the screw heads.

TIP
• Perspex is a more colourful option. Shop fitters use it and will cut it to size.

YOU WILL NEED:
- 18-mm MDF
- JIGSAW
- HACKSAW
- WORKBENCH
  OR TABLE WITH
  2 G CLAMPS
- STICKY-BACKED
  PLASTIC (OR FORMICA
  AND PANEL ADHESIVE)
- WOODEN SUPPORT
  BRACKETS
- CHROME CARPET-
  FITTING STRIP

PROJECT THREE
Creating a breakfast bar

The breakfast bar is just the thing for informal snacking. It is the very place to perch on a stool as you munch your toast and sip your espresso, or for a friend to have a drink while watching you cook. The 1950s styling means that you can have fun with the shape and cover it with shiny Formica or sticky-backed plastic sheeting, whichever the budget allows.

Breakfast bars make a convenient and space-saving place to have a snack, and this 1950s style version is fun and colourful. It can be made out of MDF and covered with Formica or sticky-backed plastic sheeting.

HOW TO DO IT

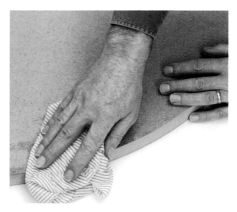

STEP 1 Draw out the shape of the pattern on the MDF. Cut the pattern out with a jigsaw. Hold the jigsaw firmly down on the surface and move with it. Sand the edge smooth, then wipe away any dust with a damp cloth.

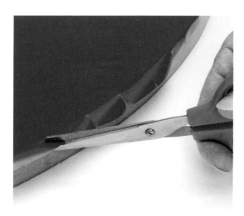

STEP 2 Cover the MDF with sticky-backed plastic, smoothing it flat as you roll it on. Snip notches on the curve of the table and fold over the edge so the plastic lays flat.

STEP 3 Cut the chrome carpet-fitting strip to size with a hacksaw.

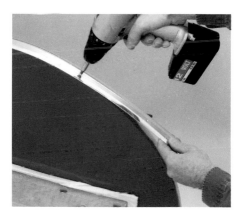

STEP 4 Drill pilot holes for the chrome strip and then into place on the edge of the table. Begin at one end of the curve, bending the strip as you go.

STEP 5 Drill holes for the bracket fittings in both the wall and MDF. Mark the position for the fittings on the wall and drill the holes. Fit the appropriate wall plugs into the holes.

STEP 6 Screw the brackets to the wall first, then screw them to the MDF. Trim the edge. Use a spirit level to check.

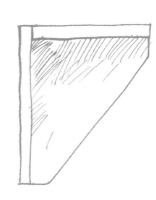

Check these illustrations when you are constructing and attaching the brackets to your kitchen wall. Always double check that they are straight with a spirit level.

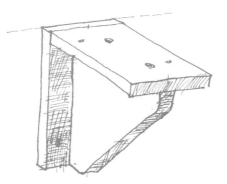

Galley kitchen

A small kitchen space should be seen as a challenge and not a problem. Believe it or not, squeezing everything into an area the size of a corridor can be an easier task than putting together a coherent style in acres of space. By using storage solutions that make the best use of the space available, galley kitchens can look extremely stylish.

Stools are an ideal seating choice for galley kitchens because although they may take up the same area of floor space as chairs, their height makes them less dense and claustrophobic.

Start by evaluating what you have in the way of major appliances such as the cooker, fridge, freezer, washing machine and tumble dryer. Some may be too big, and some you may not need at all. Do you only ever half-fill the fridge and freezer? Do you cook only under the grill, in the microwave or on the hob, and would a mini-oven be better? And do you really need a washing machine and tumble dryer? Compact versions that are more in line with your lifestyle will certainly save a lot of space and money on fuel bills. Also make sure that all the kitchen's storage potential is being used, and that there is no 'dead' space. Only keep essential equipment, and make sure that the things you use most are stored within easy reach. Remember, a galley kitchen must be functional, with as much floor space as possible, and easily accessed cupboards and appliances. A long, thin kitchen can afford to have the space trimmed down a bit and fitted with wall-to-wall shelving around the door frame. Worktops need to be kept clutter free with the food and crockery hidden behind plain doors.

Gentle variations in colour, or using the same colour for worktops, walls and units, will make the space seem bigger, and brushed steel appliances and shiny splashbacks can help by reflecting light. There is so much that can be done with a can of paint, and the new, multi-surface paints have extended these boundaries even further.

A number of important points to consider when kitchen space is tight are…

Sliding or folding doors

A door opening into a galley kitchen will be using up quite a lot of space. One way of reclaiming space is to have the door re-hung so that it opens the other way, and another is to fit a sliding door on the outside. Sliding doors still need somewhere to slide to, and if you don't have this space then think about a folding door. Concertina-style melamine panels with steel hinges look sleek, and take up only the space of the door area. Or you could make up a double-sided, heavy duty PVC curtain with eyelets, and thread it onto a chrome tube rail.

Glass shelves over windows

Kitchen windows are usually quite a generous size, which means that they eat up potential wall and storage space. If this is your problem, section off part of the window and fit it with glass shelves. The space above a window is an ideal place to store your glassware because the natural light is not completely blocked, and glasses can sparkle within easy reach.

Plain flooring

Since the overall floor area of a galley kitchen is fairly small, it should not cost the earth to invest in some very flattering floor covering. All patterned flooring follows a repeat grid of some type, and the grid pattern will visually 'shrink' the floorspace. Instead, choose a floating, wooden strip floor laid crosswise, or plain-coloured sheet lino or vinyl flooring.

Storage – everywhere

Make full use of every bit of space. Kitchen units are made to a standard depth, but most of us have things lurking towards the back that never see the light of day. Reduce the cupboard depth by 15 cm and you might have room to swing that cat! Create even more space in a shallow cupboard by fitting two shelves instead of one to make full use of the height. Fit a row of wall cupboards above eye level for things you use less often.

Task lighting

Draw the eye towards the action by lighting the worktops with an angled track of halogen spotlights. A small kitchen is no place to be stumbling about in the dark with hot oil, so make sure the work areas are bright when you need them to be. It is also best to have an ambient light source to soften the effect. Recessed, dimmable ceiling lights or even a stylish table lamp will allow for a change of atmosphere when you want it.

Expanding space with colour

When decorating a small room it is best to work with a limited palette. Use one main colour with perhaps a darker and lighter version. Earth colours work well if you have wooden doors and floors, blue is a receding colour and will 'expand' the space, and bold bright yellow is good with metal. Red will make the room look smaller but

Glass and brushed steel surfaces reflect light around a galley kitchen, helping create a bigger sense of space.

quite sexy, and white will dazzle. If you need to reflect natural light with pale walls choose cream because it looks delicious with dark wood.

Fold-away counters

Think of caravans or yachts because they provide plenty of practical inspiration for the galley kitchen. Fold-down flaps, collapsible tables, high cupboards like aeroplane lockers and pull-out bread boards are all good ideas to adapt with a touch of contemporary styling.

Stools instead of chairs

Chairs and stool legs may take up roughly the same area of floor space, but stools are less claustrophobic in galley kitchens. Perched on a high stool looking down on the worktops, the view is of the widest part of the kitchen.

Homely touches

Never forget that this galley kitchen is part of your home. Design tips can help you make the best of the space, but you should always feel free to introduce your personal style. Efficiently designed kitchens can look too clinical, so be sure to introduce some homely touches.

THE PROJECTS

The three projects on the following pages are practical, space-saving solutions that will help optimise the space in your own galley kitchen. Think about adding a few homely touches of your own to personalise the effect.

YOU WILL NEED:

• 18-MM MDF (OR
  LAMINATED WORKTOP
  OR A WIDE SHELF)
• FOLDING BRACKETS
• JIGSAW
• MEDIUM-GRADE
  SANDPAPER
• SPIRIT LEVEL
• DRILL
• MASONRY BIT (SIZE TO
  SUIT SCREWS)
• SCREWS
• SCREWDRIVER
• WALL PLUGS
• PILOT BIT
• FABLON
• PANEL PINS
• HAMMER
• NAIL PUNCH
• 25 × 25MM
  SQUARE MOULDING

PROJECT ONE

Making a hinged breakfast bar

When space is limited, it is worth thinking about when and how the room is used. There is no need to allot precious space to a permanent eating area if it is only going to be used for a quick croissant and coffee in the morning, or a bowl of noodles at night.

A fold-away bar like this one is ideal in this situation, and if you make one to match the colour of the kitchen walls, it will virtually disappear when it's not in use. Alternatively, you could choose to make a feature of it and cover it with a bright colour or pattern.

Wall-mounted, hinged breakfast bars are ideal eating areas that can be folded away after use.

HOW TO DO IT

STEP 1 Cut the MDF to the size required and cover with sticky-backed plastic, snipping and folding the corners to make a neat edge.

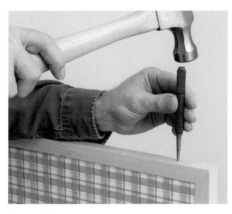

STEP 2 Cut and mitre the moulding, and use panel pins to attach it to the MDF. Use a nail punch to punch the pins home.

STEP 3 Determine the position of the shelf on the wall using a tape measure and pencil.

STEP 4 Place the shortest end of the bracket on the wall and mark screw positions. Fix and tighten all the screws.

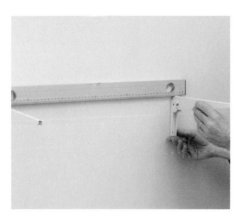

STEP 5 Align the second bracket with the spirit level. Check the horizontal. Fix the second bracket as described in step 4.

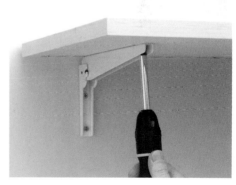

STEP 6 Fix the shelf to the brackets, leaving a 5-mm gap between the wall and the shelf for easy folding.

TIPS
- Drill a pilot hole using a 2-mm drill bit if you are screwing into MDF.
- Give up painting furniture with brushes and use small 'gloss' rollers instead. The finish is far better and you avoid the drips.
- Design the breakfast bar as an extension to the kitchen worktop so long as it doesn't block a cupboard door when folded down.

YOU WILL NEED:
- TIMBER AS FOLLOWS
  4 LEGS 50 MM x 50
  MM, 58 CM LONG;
  4 FEET 40-MM
  WOODEN KNOBS
  WITH SCREWS;
  1 BOX BASE 12-MM
  MDF, 30 CM x 30 CM;
  2 BOX SIDES 12-MM
  MDF, 30 CM x 20 CM;
  2 BOX SIDES 12-MM
  MDF, 32.5 CM x 20 CM;
  2 SEAT FRAMES 12-MM
  MDF, 30 CM x 80 CM;
  2 SEAT FRAMES 12-MM
  MDF, 32.5 CM x 80 CM;
  1 SEAT 25-MM MDF, 35
  CM x 35 CM
- PENCIL
- TAPE MEASURE
- STRAIGHT EDGE
- SAW
- WOOD GLUE
- DRILL WITH 2-MM
  BIT AND
  COUNTERSUNK BIT
- BOX OF 40-MM
  No. 6 SCREWS
- PRIMER
- PAINT
- SMALL FOAM ROLLER
  AND TRAY

PROJECT TWO
Stools for storage

Remember the space rule and don't waste an inch of it. This high stool is easy for a beginner to make, and has a useful storage box in the base. The stool can be painted to match the kitchen if you want it to blend in, or try primary colours with black legs for a Bauhaus look.

Not an inch is wasted by this high stool, which has a storage box in the base. Experiment with colours that either match or contrast with the rest of the kitchen.

HOW TO DO IT

STEP 1 Make up the two shorter sides. Drill, countersink, glue and screw the 30-cm seat frame across the top of each pair of legs. Check that the legs are square to the seat.

STEP 2 Drill, countersink, glue and screw the 30-cm box sides at the other end to overlap the ends of the legs by 12 mm and allow for the depth of the box base. Check that everything is square!

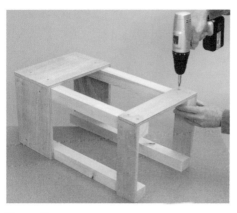

STEP 3 Join the two sides of the stool by fixing the 32.5-cm seat base and box sides between them.

STEP 4 Fix the base by screwing up into the legs from below. If this is a nice tight fit it will add stability. Fix the seat on from the top.

STEP 5 Fill all the countersunk holes with wood filler, leave to set and then sand smooth. Prime and paint the stool using a small foam roller.

STEP 6 Drill four pilot holes, then screw the wooden feet into the base.

TIPS
• You might need to plane a small amount of wood from the underneath of each of the wooden knobs that are to be used as feet. Check how the stool stands on the floor and adjust the feet accordingly.

PROJECT THREE

Fitting a rail below a floating shelf

Shelves with internal brackets give the kitchen a contemporary edge, and by fitting steel rails for cups below the shelf you can double its usefulness. If you are displaying glasses, cups or mugs in this way invest in a brand new matching set so that you can enjoy looking at them. Buy the shelves from a DIY store: they will have full fitting instructions and the fixings needed to complete the job. The design of the steel rail is best kept simple – as a rule the cheaper they are the more elaborate – so shop around for a rail that pleases the eye. Some of them can be bought complete with hooks, if not, buy blunt 'S' hooks rather than authentic butcher's hooks, which have lethal points.

Open shelves fitted with steel rails provide useful storage space without blocking out areas of the galley kitchen. Matching sets of crockery are preferable to odd sets, if you are putting them on display.

HOW TO DO IT

STEP 1 Use the tenon saw and mitre block to cut the supports for the rail.

STEP 2 Use the 22-mm spade bit to drill holes in the supports to take the rail. Drill to 15-mm depth.

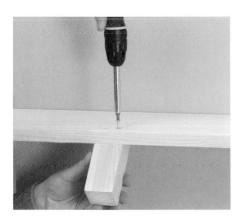

STEP 3 Drill a pilot hole through the shelf and screw the first support in place.

STEP 4 Fit the pipe into the hole of the fixed support and then fit the second support at the other end of the shelf. Screw this in position from above.

Sitting rooms

The sitting room is a space to relax, to read and to watch television. It is also the place to entertain visitors, so as the most public face of your home, it is an ideal room to reflect your personal style. This section shows you how to transform your sitting room into a choice of three different styles: Traditional, Contemporary or Global. Most sizes and shapes of sitting rooms can achieve one of these three styles, but an additional section shows you how to make the most of a small sitting room. The three step-by-step projects will start you off, and a few accessories and a fresh coat of paint will do the rest.

Traditional sitting room

The traditional sitting room is a comfort zone. A place to relax alone or with company, perhaps watch TV or listen to music, to curl up with a magazine or a good book and warm your toes in front of the open fire – somewhere to feel at home. If you live in an old building, the shape and height of the room probably suggest that you decorate it in a traditional way. Begin by choosing the right colours. Most paint companies now have a range of historical colours that are suited to different decorative periods. You don't have to recreate the past, but getting the colours right can make a huge difference to a room.

Comfortable sofas, colourful rugs and a generous scattering of cushions make the traditional sitting room a comfort zone.

The great thing now is that we have so much choice, not only in colour schemes but also in lighting, furniture and accessories. Gas-fuelled open fires are more realistic than ever, and whether you're after chandeliers or gilded mirrors, you will find excellent reproduction versions in department stores or the genuine article in antique markets. If it's out there somewhere, there will very likely be a directory to help you find it.

One very good reason for decorating a sitting room in a traditional style is that you can mix old and new pieces of furniture. Furniture is passed down through families and whether they are priceless antiques or simply granny's standard lamp, they give a home a sense of history. And if the idea of granny's lamp fills you with horror, remember it can always be repainted and treated to a new lampshade. Comfortable old sofas can be re-upholstered or dressed up with colourful throws and cushions. Try mixing old with new even if you have to cheat and buy your 'family heirlooms' from a flea market. They are often exactly what a traditionally decorated sitting room needs to settle it down, and turn it into that comfort zone. Ten points to consider that will help you to get the look are…

Open fireplace

There was a time when fireplaces were boarded up because they were too old fashioned for the modern home. They were soon opened up, however, because sitting rooms seemed so much colder and less inviting without them. If you have the real thing, dress it up with a full log basket, a coal bucket and a range of fire implements. Victorian and Edwardian-style fireplaces are still made from the original designs, and today some of them don't even need a chimney. They can be gas fuelled and lit from the comfort of your armchair via a remote control!

Fitted carpets

A traditional sitting room can have polished floorboards with a scattering of rugs or good old fitted carpets. Hard floors are fashionable at the moment, but you really can't beat wall-to-wall carpets for warmth and comfort. Choose a warm neutral colour or a woven natural material like seagrass or coir matting which matches most furniture styles.

Armchairs

There are lots of comfortable armchairs that look pretty dreadful, and fabulous-looking armchairs that weren't meant to be sat in. You should strike a balance, but looks must come into the equation. A brand new armchair can cost almost as much as a sofa, so look out for a second hand bargain. Give an old chair new life by re-upholstering it to suit the rest of the furniture.

Rugs and cushions

Rugs are like pictures on the floor. They don't have to cost a fortune but can become the focal point in a room. Plain floors can be brightened up with splashes of colour, and rugs also provide soft islands of comfort on hard wooden floors. Cushions do the same job on furniture. Don't be mean with them – the more the merrier!

Throws

Throws are not really a new invention, they are just blankets with a new name. We have all been liberated by them though, no doubt about it! Before the throw came along there was no alternative but to send for the steam cleaners or to re-upholster when accidents happened, but now we chuck on a throw and hide a multitude of sins. Throws can also introduce strong, contrasting colours, and create a more casual, relaxed and informal look.

Curtains

'Grown-up' curtains can be terribly expensive, and choosing the fabric is the only exciting part of the experience. The linings, weights, tracks and hooks are not at all thrilling and they can be seriously expensive. This does explain the popularity of curtain poles and tab-tops, which are simplicity itself to put up. Buy them ready made for convenience or buy fabric and make them yourself. If you still long for a serious set of curtains there are specialist second-hand curtain dealers who are not cheap, but you do get totally authentic grandeur.

Framed photographs, paintings and prints

Traditional sitting rooms need art on the walls. This gives you something to look at while you

The traditional sitting room mixes the old with the new, so it is an ideal place to arrange your family heirlooms (even if you have to cheat and buy them from a flea market).

them actually flatter the room. It is difficult to get the proportions right, and the light is very often far too bright, which creates a stark atmosphere. Large table lamps are better all round. They can sit on tables and cast a warm glow onto the seating area. Picture lights or wall uplighters can be used to supply more ambient light to the room.

Comfortable sofas

There are so many cheap sofas and special offers in the shops, but for the traditional look it makes more sense to wait until sale time and spend as much as possible on a quality piece of furniture in a traditional design, such as a Chesterfield. If you don't mind buying second-hand it is worth checking out local furniture auctions. They can be great fun and you never know what you might find. Factory outlets are also worth investigating because many sell end of lines and uncollected special orders at knock-down prices.

Book shelves

Restaurants, pubs and hotels have recently caught on to the fact that rows of books make the place feel like home. Fit a row of shelves into an alcove, and make a display of your books. You can cheat a bit as well – think of them as accessories and buy sets of second-hand books for their bindings. Book spines can be very decorative and charity shops always have loads of hardbacks to choose from.

Wall uplighters and large table lamps are far better methods of lighting than central ceiling lights. They cast a warm, ambient light over the room.

are relaxing, and to talk about when friends drop by. Don't worry if you don't know your Picasso from your Leonardo, you can always cheat a little. Buy old frames from a flea market and revitalise them with gilding cream or an antique gold spray paint. Frame mirrors, prints, photocopied drawings or etchings, old black and white photographs and don't forget to keep a look out for an original masterpiece.

Lighting

Most sitting rooms have central lights which hang down from the ceiling, but very few of

THE PROJECTS

The four projects on the following pages will help achieve a traditional feel to your own sitting room by adding soft, cosy furnishings on top of your existing items. Some old-framed mirrors and prints with some warm lighting will do the rest.

PROJECT ONE

Throws

YOU WILL NEED:
- 2 CONTRASTING PIECES OF FABRIC ABOUT 1.5 M SQUARE (IF THE FABRIC IS TOO NARROW, STITCH 2 WIDTHS TOGETHER AND USE THIS MEASUREMENT FOR THE LENGTH AS WELL)
- TAPE MEASURE
- SCISSORS
- PINS
- SEWING MACHINE
- THREAD
- EDGE TRIMMING

A throw is quite simply the most versatile of all soft furnishings. They are usually square but there are no size or fabric restrictions. When it comes to throws anything goes! Make a double-thickness throw using fabrics with contrasting textures and colours. This could be velvet and corduroy, fleece and cotton, or perhaps a colour co-ordinated patterned or plain fabric. Add extra style around the edge with a fringed, beaded or blanket-stitched border.

A new throw is a cheap and easy way to transform an elderly sofa or armchair, and can add a splash of warm colour to the sitting room.

HOW TO DO IT

STEP 1 Trim the patterned fabric so it is 50 mm smaller than the plain fabric. Pin the two pieces together. Mitre the corners.

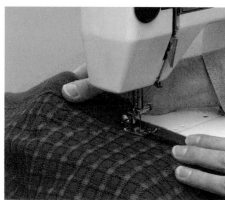

STEP 2 Sew a double row of stitches about 15 mm in from the edge, but leave a 30-mm opening in the middle of one side. Turn the fleece over to form a border and zigzag the two together along the joining edge.

TIPS
- A dark-coloured brushed cotton sheet is soft and wide, and makes a good lining fabric.
- If you have never sewn with fleece, try it! It is wide, inexpensive, the edges don't fray, it washes brilliantly and comes in a fabulous range of colours.
- Good decorative touches include tassels, buttons, twisted cord, piping or a beaded fringe.

YOU WILL NEED:

• CUSHION PAD,
  FEATHER OR
  POLYESTER FILLED
• FABRIC
• PINS
• TAPE MEASURE
• THREAD
• SEWING MACHINE

PROJECT TWO

Cushions

A chair or sofa will always look more inviting if it's stacked with plumped-up cushions. Neutral, plain-coloured covers for sofas and chairs are the most popular choice because furniture is a major expense and we want something that won't date. Cushions can be much more frivolous. A new cushion cover is quick, easy and inexpensive to make, especially if you buy remnants of luxurious fabrics. These leftovers are sold at a fraction of the original price.

A splash of strong colour on a neutral-coloured sofa in the form of plumped-up cushions creates an inviting and cosy look.

HOW TO DO IT

STEP 1 Cut one square of fabric to be the front of the cushion. Cut two pieces to overlap each other at the back. These two must measure as wide as the first square but only be two thirds as long.

STEP 2 Turn back and zigzag a small hem along one edge of each of the smaller pieces. These two seams will overlap at the back of the cushion making an 'envelope' access for the cushion pad.

STEP 3 Lay the square flat with the right side facing upwards. Place the two shorter pieces face down on it, one at each end so that they overlap one another in the middle, with the hem-stitched edges facing upwards. Piped cord can also be sandwiched in at this stage, with the flat edge facing outwards. Pin all round the edge.

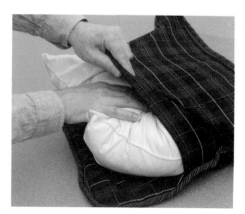

STEP 4 Sew the pieces together, about 15 mm inside the outer edge. Turn the cushion cover the right side out and press with an iron. Place the cushion pad inside the cover. For most fabrics the overlap will not need any additional fixings but soft, silky fabrics will hold their shape better with a press stud, ribbon tie or Velcro dot attached inside the overlap.

PROJECT THREE

Curtain treatments

Let the proportions of your room and the size of your windows be the deciding factor when you choose your curtain style. A large, high-ceilinged room with a bay window can look fabulous with a heavy pelmet and pleated drapes, but a smaller room would be overwhelmed by this sort of treatment and needs something lighter. A combination of plain blinds and fabric draped over a curtain pole can provide the best of both worlds. The window panes are covered by the blinds, while the hard lines of the frames are softened by the drapes.

If you have double glazing and don't need curtains for warmth, a curtain rod with ring clips is the quickest solution. The row of clips is snapped on at regular intervals and will hold most light to medium-weight fabrics. Sheets, saris and even large tablecloths can make the most elegant curtains. The project shows how to make simple tab-top, banner-style curtains.

Tab-topped curtains give a lighter effect than pelmets and pleats, so they are ideal for slightly smaller rooms and windows. Choose between a wooden or iron pole.

HOW TO DO IT

STEP 1 Measure and cut out the curtain panels and matching lining. Tab tops do not need to be much wider than the actual window width because they hang almost flat when pulled. Cut out tabs 3 cm wide and 12 cm long. Calculate how many you need, spacing them 15 cm apart. Cut out the same shape and number of strips of fabric stiffener, and iron it to the wrong side of the tabs. Iron a 5-cm-wide strip of stiffener to the wrong side of the top edge of each curtain panel.

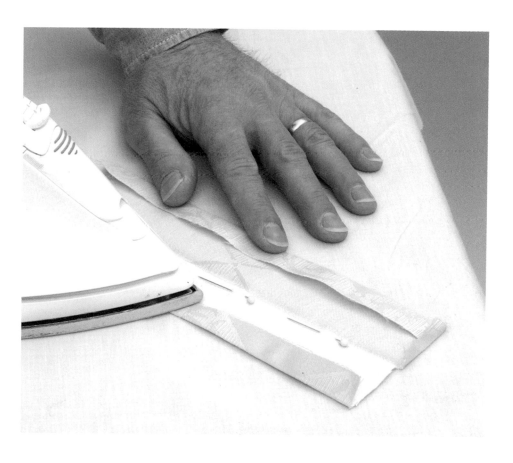

STEP 2 Sew the tabs into tubes with the stiffener on the outside. Turn them inside out and press flat. Fold each tab in half lengthways and press.

STEP 3 Pin the sides and bottom lining and fabric together with the right sides facing. Stitch around the edge and then fold the right way round. Turn the raw edges over at the top and tuck them inside. Space the folded tabs along the top edge and pin them to the stiffened fabric. Sew a double row of stitching across the top to close the seam and attach the tabs. Press the panels.

TIPS
• Stitch a button or wooden bead at the base of each loop.
• If you can't sew, buy iron-on tabs and press the seams with fabric bonding tape.
• Paint a cheap curtain pole black, and use gold leaf or paint in bands to add a touch of glamour.

YOU WILL NEED:

- 25 MM x 50 MM
  TIMBER FOR THE
  FRAMES
- TO MAKE A TWO-
  PANEL SCREEN 1.5 M
  TALL YOU NEED 13.5 M
  OF TIMBER, MITRED AS
  6 CM x 1.5 M AND 6
  CM x 75 CM
- 4 SMALL DOOR KNOBS
  FOR FEET
- MITRING SAW (OR
  HANDSAW AND
  MITRING BLOCK)
- TAPE MEASURE
- PENCIL
- WOOD GLUE
- THIN PINS
- SMALL HAMMER
- 9 x TWO-WAY HINGES
  AND SCREWS TO FIT
- BRADAWL
- SCREWDRIVER

TO FILL EACH
FRAME YOU NEED:

- PANEL OF HEAVY
  UPHOLSTERY FABRIC,
  TAPESTRY OR IKAT
  (TIE-DYED) STYLE
- STAPLE GUN
- WOOD PRIMER AND
  UNDERCOAT
- PAINT – SATINWOOD
  OR EGGSHELL FOR A
  MATT FINISH
- SMALL GLOSS ROLLER
  AND TRAY
- BRAID FOR TRIMMING
- FABRIC ADHESIVE

PROJECT FOUR

Making a two-panel screen to hide modern equipment

All your efforts to recreate the atmosphere of a traditional sitting room can be ruined by televisions, computers and video recorders. They attract the eye even when they are not switched on. Furniture stores now stock antique reproduction cabinets to conceal high-tech appliances, but they do tend to be expensive and look cheap. If you watch a lot of television it isn't practical to hide it in a cupboard, but you could take it off its stand and put it on something more in keeping with the room's style, such as a tin trunk or a wooden chest. If the room has an alcove, push the equipment back into it, and fit a wide shelf at least 30 cm above it. A blind or curtain can be fitted along the shelf edge to conceal everything when not in use. A folding screen is an even easier solution, and it also offers more decorative possibilities.

HOW TO DO IT

STEP 1 Apply wood glue to the joining edges and assemble the frames. Screw to fasten. Paint the frames and the moulding with a primer, an undercoat and the final top coat.

STEP 2 Lay the frame over the fabric and cut, leaving at least 38 mm as an overlap.

STEP 3 Stretch the fabric taut and staple it to the back of the frame. Place the first four staples halfway along each side, then staple the corners and several points in between.

STEP 4 Measure the lengths of braid needed to cover the edges. Mitre the corners then apply fabric adhesive to the back edges.

STEP 5 Lay the three screen panels flat, butted up together, and place hinges 10 cm from the top and bottom, with one in the middle. Use the bradawl to make small pilot holes for the screws.

STEP 6 Small round feet can be added using brass or wooden cupboard door knobs screwed into the base of the frames.

A folding screen is a portable and decorative way of hiding modern equipment such as computers, televisions and video recorders.

VARIATIONS
• Fit the sheets of woven cane in the same way as the fabric.
• Use small screws to secure the fretwork panels to the frames. You will need to drill clearance holes along the panel edges, and use a bradawl to make pilot holes for the screws. Paint the panels to match or contrast with the frames.

Contemporary sitting room

The really big influences over the past few years have been minimalism, modern art and eco-awareness. And a more open-plan style for living has filtered down from Manhattan lofts, while the rediscovery of 1960s high-rise apartments has found its way into everyday decorating. It is also true to say that we may not all aspire to live in converted warehouses, but we can still appreciate the clarity of an uncluttered space furnished with a few interesting pieces.

We can even try glass bricks which let light filter through to create an airy feel. In fact comfort areas are more clearly defined than ever with sheepskin rugs on hardfloors, huge sofas, low tables and lighting directed towards the seating and decorative objects. The trick is to keep colours muted and natural for a really airy feel, and introduce them by masking off and painting blocks of colour to break up the wall space. You should also add some contemporary art. This can be anything from an abstract painting to a large rock, a weather-beaten tree trunk or a large desert cactus. Just do it with confidence! Fifteen sure ways to give your sitting room a contemporary style are…

Muted, natural colours help the contemporary style by giving an airy feel. Soft throws folded over the backs of sofas add to the style.

Floating wooden floor

The new wooden floor looks different to stripped pine floorboards, the wood strips are narrower and the boards are butted up, leaving no gaps. The design principle is the same for most brands of strip flooring, although quality and price vary quite a lot. Tongue-and-groove boards are laminated with a veneer of real timber and are laid on top of existing level flooring. This sort of flooring has the look and feel of wood but is laid with the convenience of vinyl.

Glass shelving and wooden storage cubes

Glass is a strong, natural material and an essential ingredient in contemporary style. An alcove fitted with toughened glass shelves looks superb and can be used to display anything from a row of pebbles to a collection of magazines, but you will need to consider fitting concealed lighting as well. It's only when glass and light are combined that the full effect becomes clear. Use frosted glass or glass bricks as screening between rooms to create a barrier without losing the sense of space.

Eco-friendly materials

Caring about the environment means being choosy about the materials with which you decorate your home. So many chemicals infect

Wooden floors are a must in any contemporary sitting room, but new, floating wooden floors make it easier than ever before to create this look.

the air of the home these days, all in the name of treating mould, stains, bacteria and good old wear and tear. If you want a more natural environment there are organic and eco-friendly paint ranges, carpets, fabrics and cleaning materials. They will do you no harm and may prevent allergies as well.

Rugs and fabrics

Hard wooden floors give a fabulous look, but they need to be comfortable, too, especially when walking barefoot. Rugs have made a comeback recently, and all fashionable furniture outlets have ranges of colourful or neutral designer rugs, ethnic kilims, natural matting and soft sheepskins. Rugs can be used to define a seating or eating area in an open-plan room. Spend as much as you can on them and make a real feature of them by putting them on show – don't waste them under chairs and sofas! Felt, wool, mohair and rough-weave cotton are the key fabrics to use.

Blinds or sheer curtains

Contemporary window dressing has no time for flounces and frills. Fit wooden Venetian or handmade paper blinds, or hang plain, tab-topped curtains from a pole. King-size, white Egyptian cotton sheets look stunning clipped onto a rail, or if you need to inject some spicy colours, drape exquisitely embroidered sari fabrics, or hand-blocked Japanese textiles from a curtain pole. Vintage patterned fabrics and brocades combined with plain bands of colour are also very chic and stylish.

Low coffee table

A long, low coffee table looks great providing it is not piled up with clutter. Favourite styles also include designs with storage space beneath the table top. Chrome or aluminium legs with 1970s-style rosewood laminates, tubular chrome and glass, pale wood with industrial size castors, and roughly-hewn African dark wood versions are all considered to be extremely cool.

If you have the space, over-sized, dramatic house-plants like this one will add an organic feel to your contemporary sitting room, without making it seem cluttered.

Leather cushions, armchair or cube

Classic leather and chrome chairs such as the Barcelona and Wassily chairs were designed in the first half of the last century and, although they have been copied, they have never been bettered. If your finances don't stretch to a designer chair then a leather cube or even a cushion will show that you're on the right track.

Lamps and candles

Table lamps need to be quite large – think of large organic-shaped ceramic or wooden table lamps with plain, cream shades or tall and simple metal standard lamps. High-tech, tracked spotlighting systems are also fine for illuminating CD collections or books. Large multi-wick candles or tealights in a row of matching glasses are also good for creating an atmosphere.

Large, plain-coloured sofa

Big, plain-coloured sofas are very much part of the contemporary style sitting room. The most stylish sofas have a boxy shape, with ultra-generous seating and short legs. These sofas are made for putting your feet up and relaxing. Comfort is the essential antidote to all this fashionable minimalism.

Soft, folded, pashmina-style throws

The other concession to comfort comes from being able to drape your furniture and yourself in beautiful, soft woollen throws. Fold them over the arms of chairs or the back of the sofa and use them as comforters on cool nights. Pashmina shawls are the best, but anything from a fringed cot blanket, or a mohair stole, to a plaid travel rug will work if the colours are right.

Decluttering

This word may not be in the dictionary, but we all know what it means. It used to be called being neat or putting things away but now we call it 'decluttering'. There are even shops, catalogues, consultants and entire books dedicated to the art. If you have a great deal of money, you can even hire someone for £200 an hour to come round and tell you to throw out most of your stuff and put the rest of it in labelled boxes. If you would prefer a few DIY ideas, then read on...

CDs

Free up space currently used to hold your CD collection by buying a wall-mounted CD storage unit. Make sure you buy one with more space than you need. Allow for at least a third more slots than the CDs you currently own, and edit the collection as new CDs are added.

Magazines

A Perspex or bent beechwood magazine rack will look perfect, and keep magazines and colour supplements neat and tidy. Keep only the current editions in your rack and store back issues on a bookshelf in magazine box files.

Video tapes

Video tape covers are competitively garish on purpose so that they stand out from the thousands of other videos in the store. But they never look good at home, so put them away! Choose an easily accessible storage system suitable for the number of tapes you own. Woven baskets or heavy board boxes with lids are a good idea. If you own a lot of tapes, make long, plain MDF boxes with hinged flaps that can be fitted on to the wall. Use a beech or maple-veneered MDF for the front, or paint it the same colour as the walls.

Storage space down below

Choose a low table with compartments or drawers, and stand lamps on cubes or drums that can also be used to hide clutter – this only works if you go through it regularly and sort things out!

Fitted shelving units with doors and drawers

If there is one good lesson to be learned from minimalism it is that not everything is worth displaying. Choose a few decorative objects for open, glass shelves and keep the rest behind closed doors.

The contemporary sitting room is clutter-free, which requires a little day to-day discipline of putting things away behind closed doors.

THE PROJECTS

The projects on the following pages will help achieve the basic elements of any contemporary sitting room: the wooden floor and the coffee table. Some disciplined decluttering, a large, plain-coloured sofa and a big rug will do the rest.

YOU WILL NEED:

- **LAMINATED FLOORBOARDS**
- **FLOOR FITTING KIT**
- **LAMINATED FLOORING ADHESIVE**
- **FINE-TOOTHED SAW**
- **STRING LINE**
- **SPIRIT LEVEL**
- **FOAM OR FELT UNDERLAY**
- **HAMMER**
- **QUADRANT BEADING TO FIT ALONG THE SKIRTING ONCE THE FLOOR HAS EXPANDED**

PROJECT ONE

Laying a floating wooden floor

Laminated flooring is a fashion that's here to stay. It's easy to lay, looks a million dollars and is really easy to keep clean. It's made in average floorboard width and comes in a wide range of stained hardwood veneers, varying between 10 mm and 19 mm in depth. The best are the most expensive – surprise, surprise. Laminates are stain resistant, won't splinter and because of their tongue-and-groove fitting you avoid draughts coming up through gaps in the floorboards.

Existing floors need to be levelled before you begin. Concrete floors will need a heavy-duty PVC damp-proof membrane, and all floors need a good underlay of either 7 mm felt boards or 2 mm foam sheeting. When you buy laminated flooring you will also need a fitting kit and laminated flooring adhesive. The kit will contain full fitting instructions and spacers to be inserted between the floor and the skirting board because the floor will expand after it has been laid.

Laminated flooring is stain-resistant, splinter and draught-free. It comes in a range of stained veneers, the best of which are the most expensive.

HOW TO DO IT

STEP 1 Put down the underlay, butting the joints together.

STEP 2 Lay the first board with the groove on the edge next to the wall. Place spacers at the end and along the wall.

STEP 3 Lay another board loosely (without glue) at the end of the first, engaging the tongue and groove. Add another board or, depending upon the space, cut one to fit the remaining space, allowing enough room for a spacer next to the wall. Use a string line to check that the boards are straight otherwise the other boards will be out of line as well.

STEP 4 Run a continuous line of adhesive along the tongue and groove.

STEP 5 Use the tamping block with a hammer to force the boards tightly together.

STEP 6 Immediately wipe off the excess glue, which will ooze out between the joints, with a damp cloth. Begin the second row with the off-cut from the first providing it is at least 30 cm long. Lay the first three rows and leave the adhesive to dry before you continue. The last row of boards may have to be cut width-ways to fit into the space, and you must remember to allow for the spacers. Finally, remove the spacers and fit the quadrant beading to the skirting to cover the expansion gap.

Making a coffee table

YOU WILL NEED:
- 4 LENGTHS OF
  PREPARED TIMBER –
  200 x 47 MM/
  16 x 1¾ IN
- 4 BATTENS –
  50 x 22 MM/2 x ⅞ IN
- 2 SCRAPS OF SHOEBOX
  CARDBOARD
- WOOD GLUE
- 8 x 50-MM/2-IN
  No. 6 SCREWS
- 4-MM/⅛-IN DRILL BIT
- DRILL
- DARK WOODSTAIN
- BRUSH
- TAPE MEASURE
- COMBINATIONS
  SQUARE
- PENCIL
- SCREWDRIVER
- WAX POLISH
  AND CLOTH

The best coffee tables are long, low and simply elegant, the focus being on a good shape and finish. This one is made from four main pieces of prepared timber, with hidden battens to support the legs. Construction could not be more simple, and the wood can be stained deep tan or dark brown to suit the contemporary room style that has been chosen.

This long, low and elegant coffee table is easy to construct from just four main pieces of prepared timber, with hidden batons to support the legs.

HOW TO DO IT

STEP 1 Abut the four long planks of wood on a flat work surface, and lace the three scraps between them to make narrow gaps. Mark 300 mm from each end and use the combination square and a pencil to draw a line across both planks.

STEP 2 Lay out the four lengths of batten and draw in the halfway line (75 mm). Drill a hole in the middle of each half on all four pieces. Place one batten along the inside of each of the lines across the two planks. Coat the battens with wood glue and then screw them to the planks.

STEP 3 Draw a centre guideline across the width of each leg.

STEP 4 Apply a liberal coating of wood glue to the base of each of the legs and to the side of the batten then, having lined them up with the gap, put both legs in place.

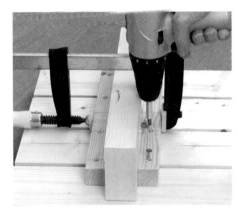

STEP 5 Now fix a second batten to the other side of the leg to hold it firmly from both sides. Apply wood glue to the surfaces and screw the battens to the planks. Leave to bond overnight. (This is very important, no matter what it says on the tube!)

STEP 6 Apply a coat or two of woodstain, tinted varnish or wax polish.

Global sitting room

This is a room where colour leads and everything else follows on. If you love colour then this is the way to proceed, and it's a very helpful approach if you are starting from scratch and don't know where to begin. Once you have decided on, say, burnt orange, pale blue and cream for the walls, then the furniture and accessories can be chosen because they look great against that background.

(Right) This Moroccan-style room displays the elaborately carved furniture and exotic colours traditional to the region.

Deep, earthy reds in a symmetrical pattern conjure up the heat of North Africa.

A colour scheme can be inspired by anything that you see about you, from a bowl of fresh fruit or flowers to your favourite sweet wrapper or the background in a holiday snap. In fact it is easier to find paint to match a colour that you have already chosen than it is to begin by staring at a paint chart for inspiration. Charts are fantastic once you know what you're looking for, but confusing when you don't.

Colour ranges get bigger, brighter and bolder all the time, and whereas a few years ago you could only buy strong colours for walls from an expensive paint specialist, they now appear in the DIY stores' own ranges at a fraction of the price. Match pots allow you to experiment with colours and are far more helpful than a small rectangle on a white background. And if you only want a small amount for an area of intense colour, they do the job at a great price.

Tricks with colour

There is no doubt that the TV decorating programmes have had a massive influence on the way we think about using colour at home. Most rules regarding good taste have been broken in the quest for more riveting TV, and this has actually been quite liberating. Now it's OK to say that you chose turquoise and lime with a splash of silver-leaf gilding because it tickled your fancy!

Also note that blocks of colour can be used to create dramatic effects in a room. As a rule red

foreshortens a room, bringing the walls in closer, while blue recedes. This is the way our eyes read these colours, and you can use them to stretch or compact a space accordingly. Play visual tricks with colour. For example, yellow lightens and brightens rooms, and is really useful when a room doesn't get much natural daylight. Colour also effects our moods, making us feel happy, tranquil, excited or irritable, which is something to bear in mind when you are doing up your global sitting room.

THE PROJECTS

Colour ranges have associations with different cultures and climates. This means that you can conjure up the mood of another place using its characteristic colours. The following three projects show how you can use colour to create an African, Moroccan or Mediterranean style. A low divan bed, rough-textured wall and a small table are the common starting points.

Cool stone floors, earthy coloured textiles in bold patterns and an open fire bring a taste of Africa to this sitting room.

YOU WILL NEED:
- PAINT
- MASKING TAPE
- BRUSHES
- DARK WOODSTAIN
- ACCESSORIES SUCH AS
  DRUMS, BEADWORK,
  EBONISED WOODEN
  MASKS, SOAPSTONE
  CARVINGS, HIDE RUGS
  AND FOLDING
  DIRECTOR'S CHAIRS

PROJECT ONE
The African room

The colours of Africa are drawn from the landscape: rusty reds and dark, mud browns of the earth, yellow ochres of the sun, and pale, sky blues are combined with the rich, ebony black of cooking pots on the open fire. The style is plain with organic shapes and bold patterns. Look out for woven and printed African textiles for throws and cushion covers, wood-carved figures, woven grass matting, clay pots, gourd bowls, and recycled African tin and wirework.

This African-style wall reflects the colours of the landscape – the rusty red of the earth the soft, yellow ochre of the sun, and the blue sky between. A woven grass mat in a bold, spiral pattern completes the effect.

HOW TO DO IT

STEP 1 Stain the floorboards using a very dark woodstain. Measure and mark 1 m up the wall from the floor and stick up a line of masking tape.

STEP 2 Paint the wall above the tape a soft, yellow ochre colour. Use random brush strokes to sweep the colour in different directions.

STEP 3 Paint from the floor to the tape in a rich earthy red.

STEP 4 Remove the tape and paint a free-hand brush line using a pale stone-coloured paint. Don't be nervous – it should look hand-painted.

STEP 5 Cover the divan with a rough-weave African cloth, tucked under tightly at the edges. Add cushions covered in dark brown and cream or indigo blue batik-patterned cottons, or fabric patterned like zebra, giraffe or leopard skin.

STEP 6 Use grass matting on the floor, baskets woven from grasses, gourd bowls, a pendant light with an African sun hat as a shade, a small table painted black and a top covered with a woven place mat.

YOU WILL NEED:
- **PAINT WITH A BLUE PIGMENT**
- **MASKING TAPE**
- **BRUSH**
- **STENCIL PAPER**
- **SCALPEL**
- **ACCESSORIES SUCH AS TOOLED LEATHER POUFFES, CAMEL SADDLE STOOLS, BEADED AND MIRRORED CUSHIONS, KAFTANS TO BE MADE INTO CUSHIONS AND ENGRAVED BRASSWARE**

PROJECT TWO
The Moroccan room

The north of Africa has an Arab culture where strong Islamic principles influence the decorative traditions. The homes have cool marble floors, arched shuttered windows and mathematical patterns everywhere. The look is exotic, mysterious and highly stylised. Look out for tasselled and mirrored textiles, kilim rugs, small, carved shelves and Ali Baba pots.

This stepped, geometric pattern border stencilled along the skirting board shows the mathematical patterns typical of the Moroccan decorative tradition. Moroccan rugs, tasselled cushions and an arched, framed mirror add to the look.

HOW TO DO IT

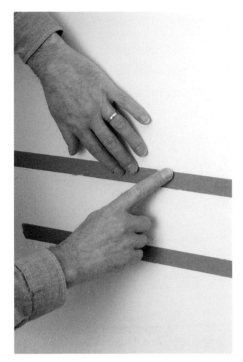

STEP 1 Mark a tile's depth white border at skirting board level.

STEP 2 Paint the wall above the border in a deep blue paint.

STEP 3 Stencil the stepped geometric pattern border along the skirting board (stencil pattern provided) in emerald green, deep red and black on white.

STEP 4 Lay Moroccan rugs and durries overlapping each other to cover the floor. Hang an arched framed mirror, beaded bags, mirrored cloth wall hangings and small carved shelves on the wall.

STEP 5 Place a date palm in an Ali Baba pot on the floor, and a large brass tray on the small table laid with a set of Moroccan tea glasses.

YOU WILL NEED:
- PAINT
- DADO RAIL
- PANEL ADHESIVE
- COUNTERSUNK
  SCREWS
- STENCIL PAPER
- SCALPEL
- BRUSH
- ACCESSORIES SUCH
  AS GERANIUMS IN
  TERRACOTTA POTS,
  BRASS OIL LAMPS,
  BLUE AND WHITE
  CUSHIONS,
  PATTERNED PLATES
  AND SMALL PICTURES
  IN FRAMES

PROJECT THREE
The Mediterranean room

There are many countries and islands around the Mediterranean Sea, and each has its own distinctive decorating style. The influence of the warm dry climate is seen in the cool interiors with tiled floors and shuttered windows. White is the dominant colour, its brilliance enhanced by the azure blue sky. The dry climate simplifies the decorating because no sealants are needed. Walls are painted with chalky distemper and wood is left unvarnished. There are different traditional embroidery, weaving, ceramic and ironwork patterns throughout the Mediterranean.

This wall has been divided using a wooden moulding, painted a deep turquoise blue. The paint above and below has a chalky texture. A group of small pictures in frames and a grapevine stencil painted along the top of the wall complete the effect.

HOW TO DO IT

STEP 1 Divide the wall at the height that a dado rail would be using a wooden moulding. This can be applied with panel adhesive and strengthened with a few countersunk screws.

STEP 2 Paint the bottom half of the wall using a pink, chalky finish paint.

STEP 3 Paint the top half with a creamy yellow, chalky finish paint.

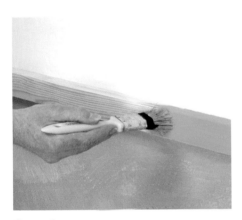

STEP 4 Paint the dado rail deep turquoise or cobalt blue.

STEP 5 Stencil a grapevine along the top of the wall. This does not have to look realistic in vine colours, just stencil it in one colour to look like a shadow in dark green or terracotta.

STEP 6 Cover the divan with a blue and white Greek embroidered bedspread, and hang up a Greek fisherman's lamp.

STEP 7 Hang a rustic unvarnished wooden shelf and a group of small pictures in frames. Cover the table with a white lace-edged cloth and a vase of bright flowers. Add red geraniums in terracotta pots, blue and white rustic ceramic wares and a rush-seated chair.

Enlarge the stencil below and transfer the pattern to plastic or stencil paper. Cut out carefully using a sharp craft knife.

Tiny sitting room

With a small room, you have to decide whether to accept it and decorate without deception, or to play tricks with colour, light and mirrors to create an illusion of a bigger space. Many flat conversions have left rooms that are either tall and narrow, or low and long, but it's amazing what a few tricks of colour, furnishing and lighting will do to change the apparent shape of the room. Whichever you choose, you will have to maximise all the space you have by organising your possessions and using every storage trick in the book, from disguised drawers to making the most of any nooks and crannies.

The first thing you need to think about is how many people will regularly use the sitting room. If it will be no more than two, then a small sofa and a place for the television, stereo and coffee table are all that's really needed. If it's more than two, you need to get creative!

Small is beautiful

If you decide to make a feature of the room's diminutive size it can be made into a very sexy, tactile space where the edges between furniture, floor and walls are blurred. Remember the shagpile carpet. It must be due for a revival and wouldn't break the bank in a tiny room; an alternative option would be a long-haired rug like the flokati, another 1970s favourite, which is handwoven with a very thick, shaggy wool pile. A low couch, felt cushions, knitted throws and fake fur rugs are other things to consider. A sheepskin-covered bean bag would be the ultimate accessory. The lower walls can either be covered with a soft-textured wallpaper or even be lined with fabric like a Bedouin tent. Emphasise the cosiness by painting the room a dark colour, such as deep red or chocolate brown, with gilded woodwork, and have plenty of warm, low lighting and thick curtains. Vintage velvets, draped felt or dyed blankets buttoned over a pole all work well.

Think big

If you decide that the challenge is to make everyone believe that the room is twice its actual size, then your first accessory has to be a mirror. If an entire wall is lined with mirror tiles the room will appear double its size, but there are more subtle ways of using mirrors that will make the space appear bigger, and make the shape look more interesting as well. You will need to watch the lighting though, as the reflections can be blinding. A pair of wooden window frames fitted with mirrors will give the appearance of looking into another room, long mirrors placed across the corners of the room will make it look octagonal, and a large, arched, framed mirror will appear to be a doorway into an adjoining room. Plants in front of mirrors will also look twice as bushy thanks to the reflection. Use pale colours, playing around with two or three different tones of yellow, light blue or green. The deeper shades will appear to recede and give shape to flat walls.

Doors and windows

Windows are best played down by fitting blinds or shutters into the frame. Keep the colour the same or lighter than that of the walls. A half-glazed door or a window onto a passage way is a means of including the space outside the room.

You can make a feature out of a small room like this one by deciding firmly what it will be used for before you start. This one is definitely a reading room. A long, low couch in neutral colours blends into the surrounding walls. Floor-to-ceiling book-cases complete the look.

And if you could do without the door altogether, it could be removed to give a more open-plan feel to the room.

Tall rooms

In old buildings that have been converted into flats, the ceilings are often very high. This is fabulous when the room is in proportion, but all too often large reception rooms have been sectioned off and the resulting rooms are narrow and tall. There are a few simple tricks though, which will help to squash the room into shape. Paint the ceiling and cornice down to picture rail height using a dark matt colour. Hang the lights so that they emerge below this level and cast the light downwards. Use a patterned carpet or rugs to attract the eye downwards, and hang pictures a bit lower than you normally would. If you would prefer to do something more substantial, why not build a

platform to raise one half of the room up to a different level? This would create useful storage space at the same time.

Short rooms

If your tiny room has a low ceiling and you need to raise the roof then similar tricks can be used in reverse. Vertical stripes have an elongating effect, and a white ceiling with no centre light will give the room a lift. Use spotlights to pick out pictures or interesting objects, and wall uplighters for ambient light.

THE PROJECTS

The projects on the following pages show two ways of making the most of a small room. The first uses an aluminium-leaf wall to make a room look bigger, and the second shows how to make a drawer disguised as part of the skirting board.

YOU WILL NEED:

• SILVER MATT
  EMULSION PAINT,
  WHICH MUST BE
  WATER-BASED

• ALUMINIUM LEAF
  (SOLD IN ART SHOPS
  GENERALLY IN PACKS
  OF 25 SQUARE LEAVES)

• WATER-BASED GOLD
  SIZE (GLUE)

• GLOSS OR SATIN
  VARNISH

• ROLLER AND TRAY

• PAINT BRUSH

• SOFT CLOTH

• LONG RULER

PROJECT ONE

Covering a wall with foil squares

A surface that reflects light will blur the boundaries as well. This project shows how to use squares of aluminium leaf to create a glowing wall in a small room. If you like the idea but would find a whole wall overpowering, why not begin by lining an alcove? Silver looks good with pale wood, frosted glass and smart navy blue furniture.

An aluminium-leaf wall reflects the colours around it, blending into the walls on either side.

HOW TO DO IT

STEP 1 Apply two coats of silver paint to the wall, allowing the correct drying times before and after the second coat.

STEP 2 Measure out a section of wall big enough for nine squares and apply the glue. Leave it for about 15 minutes until it feels tacky. Begin applying the leaf in one of the top corners, pressing the square gently onto the wall and rubbing the back lightly with your fingers.

STEP 3 Slowly peel the backing paper off from top to bottom. If any of the leaf remains on the paper, replace it and rub the back again lightly. Line the next square up to the edge of the first. Continue in the same way, fitting the squares in sections until the wall is covered.

STEP 4 Buff the leaf to a gleaming shine using a lint-free soft cloth. Apply a coat of satin or gloss varnish to protect your work of art.

YOU WILL NEED:

- 8 SMALL CASTORS
- LENGTH OF SKIRTING BOARD TO MATCH THE EXISTING ONE (IF IT CAN'T BE RE-USED)
- PANEL ADHESIVE
- 50 x 25 MM BATTEN
- 12-MM MDF SHEET FOR SHELF
- 6-MM MDF FOR DRAWER BASE
- 6-MM MDF FOR 4 DRAWER SIDES
- HANDSAW
- THIN PANEL PINS
- SMALL HAMMER
- PAINT AND A BRUSH
- SPIRIT LEVEL
- DRILL
- MASONRY BIT
- WALL PLUGS

PROJECT TWO

Disguised storage

If you really want to disguise something the trick is to make it look the same as everything around it. This project does this by building a boxed-in shelf with a drawer at floor level, and using a skirting-board front to disguise it so well that it could almost be used as a safe. This is also a way to make the most of an alcove by building the shelf wide enough for the TV. If the alcove is not deep enough it will need to be built out at the front, but the basic idea remains the same.

This drawer on castors has been built as part of a low, boxed-in shelf, and disguised with a skirting-board front to blend in with the edges around it.

HOW TO DO IT

STEP 1 Measure the depth of the alcove. If it needs extending, take this into account and cut out 2 side pieces of 25 x 50mm to support the shelf. If the shelf height is 500 mm the sides will need to be 488 mm. Drill and screw to the wall and then check the level.

STEP 2 Cut the shelf to fit the alcove. Cut a U-shaped cable hole on the back edge. Apply a long bead of adhesive to the top edges of the sides and place the shelf on top. Use a hammer to drive in some thin pins to hold the shelf securely. If the alcove is wide, add a supporting leg to the middle.

STEP 3 Make up the two drawers: cut the base of each drawer to fit snugly inside the alcove allowing just enough clearance for it to slide in and out without catching.

STEP 4 Cut drawer sides to match the depth of the shelf, and a front and back to be butted into them.

STEP 5 Fit four castors to the base of each drawer.

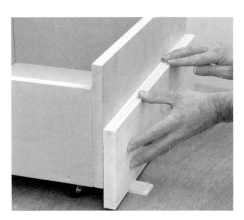

STEP 6 Cut the skirting board to fit onto the drawer front (and box sides if the shelf has been built out beyond the alcove). Stick the skirting board onto the drawer front (and box sides if built out) with panel adhesive. Do this so that the skirting board skims the floor, hiding the castors. Paint the sides and front of the drawers to match the walls and the skirting to match the skirting board.

Dining rooms

Good food, good wine and good company are made even more special by a stylish dining room, but even the simplest of meals can be made into a special occasion by a beautiful setting. Since the dining room is all about eating, much of the style is down to the table and chairs, but flooring, lighting and colour can have just the same impact. This section shows you how to transform your dining room into one of three different styles: Traditional, Contemporary or Sitting-dining room. The step-by-step projects will start you off, and a fresh coat of paint and some flexible lighting should do the rest.

Traditional dining room

The dining room is the place to indulge yourself. There was a time when most family life took place here – meals were eaten around the table, and that was also where children played and did their homework. Fashions change though and after the 1960s homes were built with dining areas rather than whole dining rooms. In older houses internal walls were knocked down to make kitchens bigger, and after that walls were knocked down between living rooms and dining rooms as well to make even larger open-plan spaces. Dining rooms became something of a luxury because only people with large houses still had them.

Wooden chairs with upholstered seats can be revamped with a fresh coat of paint and a change of fabric.

It has taken a while but with the top two leisure activities now being cooking and decorating, there has been a natural progression towards reinstating the dining room. It is now thought extremely stylish to invite your guests into your dining room to serve them a lovely meal without a television or kitchen sink in sight. Traditional dining rooms also make it a lot easier to cheat with the cooking when the chef is out of sight next door.

Chairs

The key ingredients in a classy dining room are the chairs. You can always fake the table by using an elegant tablecloth to cover an old door on trestles, but the chairs will be on show and should be as good looking and as comfortable as they possibly can be.

The great thing about opting for the traditional style is that you can always pick up second-hand dining room chairs for a reasonable price in flea markets or at an auction. The trick is to buy them one, two or three at a time, because they are always much cheaper than in sets of four or more. They don't even have to match so long as they are of more or less the same period and style. In fact, a slightly mismatched collection of chairs can look really chic if you decorate them in the same way.

The Swedish Gustavian style is well suited to this treatment, and it is a classic look that manages to appear traditional and fresh at the same time. Paint the woodwork matt white and give it a 'mildly distressed' look by rubbing the paint back to the bare wood in places with sandpaper. The seats can be covered with a red, yellow or blue gingham or stripe.

Wooden chairs with upholstered seats can easily be given a whole new style with a change of fabric and a lick of paint. Strip the wood of its old varnish and re-stain it a deep rich brown, and then cover the seats with a warm-coloured velvet or brocade fabric. Look out for remnants of good quality upholstery fabric or even old curtains which are often abandoned when people move house, and find their new homes have different shaped windows.

Tables

Tables are usually expensive and are one of the few pieces of furniture that seem to hold their value whether they are in fashion or not. Choose a table with the right proportions for your room – there must be enough space for you to move

A chandelier over the dining table is the centre-piece to the traditional dining room. Traditional-style, matching cutlery, linen serviettes and fresh flowers add a finishing touch.

around it, pull out the chairs and serve a meal without having to hug the wall. Most traditional dining tables have hidden fold-out flaps so that they can expand from four or six to eight or ten settings. They are ideal for occasional entertaining. The only other furniture needed in a dining room is a console table, sideboard or trolley for the food.

Colours

Colours can be rich, strong and dramatic in dining rooms. Hang large-framed pictures and mirrors on the walls and go to town with the curtains and lighting as well. If you own a chandelier, then this is the place to use it. Candlelight turns a meal into an occasion, and a candelabra hung over the table will bring an air of grandeur to even the simplest of meals. Keep a look out for an old chandelier in a flea market – it will often need mending and rewiring but it will be worth it.

If the room is warm enough to do without a carpet then why not try stencilling a border pattern on the floor? This is a good way to get the unifying look of an expensive carpet at a fraction of the price. There are some fabulous stencil patterns on the market, and with a few pots of stencil paint and a dash of confidence you could paint anything from a simple folk art border to a very convincing Turkish carpet in your spare time. And don't forget the finishing touches – a smooth white tablecloth with matching serviettes, traditional-style cutlery, sparkling glassware and a vase of fresh flowers.

THE PROJECTS

The two projects on the following pages show how to paint broad, vertical stripes in the traditional style, and how to revamp old dining chairs in the Gustavian (Swedish) style, complete with new, matching upholstery.

YOU WILL NEED:

- SMALL SPONGE
  ROLLER AND TRAY
  FOR THE STRIPES
- 2 COLOURS OF
  EMULSION PAINT
- WALLPAPER PASTE
  (MIXED)
- 2.5-CM PAINT BRUSH
- ROLLER AND TRAY
  FOR THE
  BACKGROUND
- MASKING TAPE
- FOAM WASHING-UP
  SPONGE
- PLUMB LINE (STRING
  AND A KEY WILL DO
  THE JOB)
- LONG RULE WITH
  SPIRIT LEVEL
- PENCIL

PROJECT ONE

Painting broad stripes with a roller

There is no need to be restrained just because you have decided to decorate the dining room in a traditional style. If you are doing French Empire style, the stripes can be broad, bold, black and gold; if your theme is Swedish, make them yellow and grey. Arts and Crafts colours are earthy, woody green and rust red. Every traditional style has certain key patterns and colours, and these stripes are a quick and easy way to give your room a dramatic new look.

Broad, vertical stripes painted in colours to suit a particular traditional style are an easy way to give your dining room a completely new look.

HOW TO DO IT

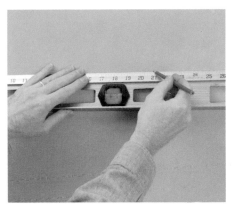

STEP 1 Decide whether you want the stripes to go the full length of the wall or just up to the picture rail. Here we are painting a horizontal stripe at picture rail height. Room heights vary, so judge this by eye. Hang the plumb line above the height of the stripe, and use the rule to mark the stripe's position along the wall.

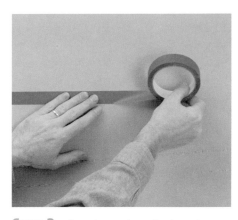

STEP 2 Follow the marks with a line of masking tape between the corners. Paint the lighter background colour between the skirting board and the tape, and leave to dry.

STEP 3 Put the second colour in the small roller tray and mix it half and half with pre-mixed wallpaper paste. Run the roller through the paint until evenly coated.

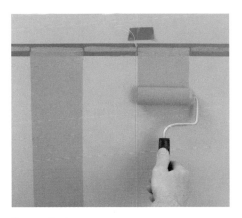

STEP 4 Make a stripe guide by marking the masking tape with the roller, leaving a roller's width between the stripes.

STEP 5 With the plumb line as a guide run the roller down the wall in a straight line. Do not press too hard, but keep the pressure even. Stop just short of the skirting board and re-charge the roller. Continue in this way, moving the plumb line as you progress so that you don't drift off the vertical.

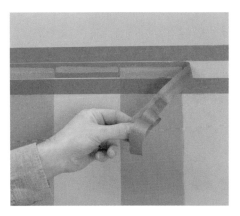

STEP 6 When the wall is finished, dip the small sponge into the paint and use it to stamp the rest of the line up to the skirting board (the roller will not reach this last bit).

STEP 7 Remove the masking tape and leave the paint to dry. Now run a line of masking tape with its top edge along the top of the stripes and then another 50 mm above it. Check it with the spirit level.

STEP 8 Use the brush to paint inside the masking tape using the striping colour, or a contrasting colour to match the skirting board if you prefer. Peel away the tape when the paint has dried.

YOU WILL NEED:

- **CHAIR WITH A PADDED SEAT, EITHER DROP-IN OR FIXED**
- **PAINT AND VARNISH STRIPPER**
- **PAINT BRUSH**
- **NEWSPAPER**
- **RUBBER GLOVES**
- **SCRAPER**
- **WIRE WOOL**
- **WHITE SPIRIT**
- **MATT WHITE PAINT**
- **CANDLE**
- **PAINT BRUSH OR SMALL FOAM ROLLER AND TRAY**
- **SANDPAPER**

PROJECT TWO

Doing up a dining chair

Everyday furniture used to be far better made than it is now, so it really makes sense to buy a selection of old dining chairs with drop-in or upholstered seats. These are not expensive antiques, but chairs from the days when every home had a dining room table and chairs. A tall-backed design is best for this Gustavian (Swedish) style, and it is amazing how much of a set an odd bunch will look once they have been given a similar paint finish and upholstery.

Old dining chairs can be transformed into this Gustavian style using a distressed paint finish and reupholstering in red, yellow or blue gingham, or stripes.

HOW TO DO THE PAINTING

STEP 1 Put on the rubber gloves and stand the chair on newspaper. Cover it in a thick coating of paint stripper and wait for the surface to bubble up.

STEP 2 Scrape off the paint or varnish, taking care to drop all the waste onto the newspaper.

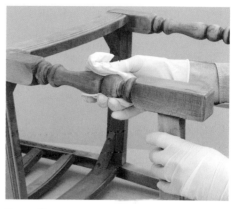

STEP 3 Dip the wire wool in white spirit and clean off the remaining paint or varnish. Leave to dry.

STEP 4 Rub the edges of the chair and any raised pattern on the wood, the curve of the legs and the seat corners with the candle. A light stroke will be enough.

STEP 5 Apply two coats of the white paint, allowing the correct drying time between and after.

STEP 6 Rub the waxed areas with sandpaper. The paint should lift away easily, so that the bare wood shows through in places. It is important not to overdo this effect because it is meant to simulate natural wear and tear.

YOU WILL NEED:

- LONG-NOSED PLIERS
- CALICO
- CHECKED FABRIC
- STAPLE GUN OR TACKS AND A SMALL UPHOLSTERY HAMMER
- BRAID FOR EDGING (OPTIONAL)
- FABRIC GLUE
- PINS

HOW TO DO THE UPHOLSTERY

STEP 1 Strip off the old fabric and remove the old tacks and staples. Replace the seat pad if necessary.

STEP 2 Lay the calico over the seat and cut it to fit, allowing enough to fold down the sides and turn over a small hem.

STEP 3 Use the calico as a template and cut out the checked fabric adding an extra 20 mm on all sides so that it will overlap the calico on the seat. Turn over and press a small hem on both pieces.

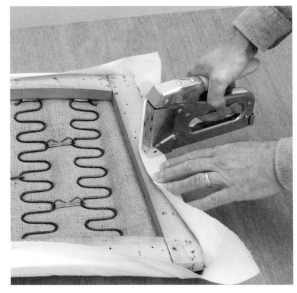

STEP 4 Lay the calico over the seat and fix it to the frame in the middle of one side first, then stretch it across and staple it in the middle of the opposite side. Do the same with the back and front.

STEP 5 Fold a triangle under at each corner and staple this flat to the frame on both sides. Do this on opposite corners, and then pleat the excess fabric over and staple it to the frame. Fix the calico all the way around the seat.

STEP 6 Fix the checked fabric to the seat in the same way. It should be fixed a bit lower than the calico so that it covers it completely, which also means that the staples will not conflict. If using braid, apply a continuous bead of glue to the back and, working from the centre back, place the braid over the line of staples along the edge of the fabric. Pin to hold it in place until the glue has bonded.

Contemporary dining room

Fabulous contemporary restaurants provide terrific inspiration, and what a tasty way to research a look! The look is essentially pared down, clean and uncluttered. The materials are natural and the line is simple. With this sensual style any unnecessary decoration has been removed to be replaced with space, texture and clarity.

Some style magazines have named this 'hotel chic' and there is an element of truth in the tag. But don't be put off: the hotels they refer to are top-of-the-range, contemporary establishments. They are more like lifestyle palaces where those in the know choose to gather and socialise. Luckily for the rest of us, designs filter down faster than ever now, and most top styles can be recreated and accessorised at a fraction of the original cost. Everyone's doing it, and it's a lot more fun than being conventional. The nine key ingredients include…

Glass

A sheet of tempered tinted glass resting on a pair of trestles looks cool and makes a practical dining surface. It is easy to clean, won't scratch and costs less than wood. Suitable toughened glass with rounded corners and smooth edges can be ordered to size from a local glazier, and several contemporary furniture stores sell pairs of suitable trestles.

Wood

Dark stained wood has staged a comeback. If you can't afford the real thing, you can buy a sheet of 25-mm MDF and give it a rosewood finish with the help of some deep, red-brown paint and a rubber graining tool. Supported on trestles, the finish is amazingly realistic, and if you splash out on a sheet of glass to cover the tabletop nobody will be able to tell the difference.

Buying second-hand

Look out for second-hand furniture that can be updated with a dark stain. The lines must be squared off and boxy, with straight or tapered legs. If you have a large room check out second-hand office furniture dealers who sometimes have boardroom tables and chairs for sale. This is a way to get top-quality furniture at a very low price. And if you're not ready for dark wood or simply prefer a lighter look, then go for pale ash or beech with straight legs and squared-off edges.

Stainless steel

Stainless steel in the dining room is fine in small doses, for example, handles on the sideboard, cutlery, lampshades and the pepper grinder and saltcellar, otherwise it will begin to look industrial. The trick is to get a balance between the hard and soft edges in the room. Keep it cool but comfortable.

Floors

Carpets are something of a liability when food and wine are being consumed. The best flooring in the contemporary dining room is a floating wooden floor. The least expensive laminated types are fine for a dining room and are guaranteed to be stain-resistant. If you can't decide between dark and light wood, then why not alternate them? Floor strips laid in stripes of different shades make a really bold, contemporary statement.

The best flooring in a contemporary dining room is a floating wooden floor. The cheapest laminated types are good enough for the dining room, alternated dark and light strips of wood give an effective look.

Chairs

There are many superb modern chairs to choose from, and the key questions to ask are how often you will be using them and for how many hours at a time. If there are just two of you most of the time, it makes sense to buy two really good chairs and a set of four others that will look good, but which won't break the bank. If you entertain a lot then bite the bullet and buy a matching set of modern upholstered chairs because they are definitely the most comfortable.

Children

If children are going to use the dining room every day, the chairs need to be resilient and easy to clean. Shiny wooden floors can be dangerous for children who rock back on their chairs, so fit rubber tips on wooden chair legs or, better still, buy moulded polypropylene or plywood chairs with tubular steel legs, which are always rubber tipped. And, since sitting at the table should never seem like hard work for kids, buy a generously sized, brightly coloured PVC cloth to protect the tabletop so that everyone can relax.

Lighting

The table is the only area that needs to be fully lit. The lighting should be good enough for everyone to see what they're eating without shining in anyone's eyes and blinding them, or being too ambient and not casting enough light. Consider frosted glass wall lights, which can be used to provide an ambient glow, table lamps to add diffused light and halogen spotlights directed on to the serving area or sideboard. And the table? You can't go wrong with candles. Look for the most contemporary styles such as long rectangular blocks with six or more wicks, tall tapers or clear glass tubes. There are so many to choose from.

Colour

Choose a harmonious colour scheme avoiding strong contrasts, but this doesn't mean it has to be safe or dull. Textured paint could be applied to one or two walls to give a linen, suede, rustic or metallic effect. If you are searching for colour inspiration, have a look in a contemporary cookbook. A café au lait with a slice of chocolate cake would give you cream, tan or dark brown, and tandoori chicken with lime pickle and poppadums would give you deep red, burnt orange and pale yellow. It's not a bad way to plan the dining room colour scheme!

THE PROJECTS
The two projects on the following pages show how to make a concealed wall uplighter for subtle, ambient lighting, plus a rosewood-effect dining table out of MDF.

A sheet of toughened glass on a trestle makes a stunning contemporary dining table. The glass can be ordered to size from a glazier, with the corners rounded and the edges smoothed.

PROJECT ONE

Mood lighting using a concealed uplighter

Instead of buying several feature wall lights, this project shows how to make an uplighter that is fixed on the wall and painted to blend into it. It is in effect an upside-down pelmet which conceals one or more slimline fluorescent striplights as a low-voltage wall light. Make the box unit to fit the length of wall, or just long enough for a single light fitting (like the fittings usually used below kitchen cupboards). Get a qualified electrician to insert the wiring into the wall; any additional fittings can use the box so that only one wall access point is needed.

This subtle uplighter is made out of MDF and painted the same colour as the wall behind. Behind it is a slimline fluorescent striplight. The uplighter can be made to fit a single light fitting, like this one, or made to fit the length of a whole wall.

HOW TO DO IT

STEP 1 Mark the position for the 50 mm x 25 mm batten on the wall. Ideally this should be at eye level so that the tubes are completely concealed by the front plate.

STEP 2 Locate the studs in the wall and fix the batten into them using the 50-mm screws.

STEP 3 Fix the shelf to the batten, at a right angle to the wall, using 40-mm screws.

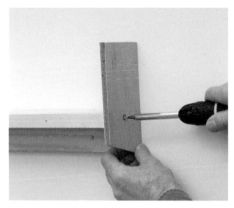

STEP 4 Place the end plates in position, and mark the angle to be cut away between the front and the batten. Use a saw to cut the angle, then fix the end plates in position.

STEP 5 Fix the MDF front plate to the shelf front using a 40-mm screw every 100 mm.

STEP 6 Prime the unit then paint it using the same colour as the wall behind. Place the light fitting inside the unit and connect the wiring as necessary. There is no need to fix the light fitting inside the unit.

YOU WILL NEED:

- SHEET OF 25-MM MDF
- PVA
- PAINT BRUSH
- DEEP RED-BROWN VINYL SILK AS THE BASE COLOUR
- SMALL FOAM ROLLER AND TRAY
- WATER-BASED CLEAR GLAZE
- TUBE OF BLACK ACRYLIC PAINT TO TINT THE GLAZE (OR BLACK INK)
- 50-MM BRUSH
- RUBBER OR PLASTIC GRAINING ROLLER
- SOFT COTTON CLOTH
- PLASTIC CONTAINER FOR THE GLAZE
- CLEAR MATT VARNISH

PROJECT TWO

Rosewood graining an mdf table top

Rosewood has a deep red base with a dramatic near-black grain. The real thing is very expensive but it is actually quite easy to fake with the aid of a rubber graining roller. This can be bought in specialist paint stores and even some DIY chainstores. MDF is an ideal material for this treatment because it has a perfectly smooth surface with no grain of its own. Buy a sheet of 25-mm MDF cut to a size that will suit your room and the number of people you need to seat, and support it on trestles. If you have never tried woodgraining before, don't be put off, it is not as technical as it appears. You will need to practise with the graining tool and glaze, however, before you paint the table. You will soon discover the right amount of glaze needed and the technique for rocking the roller as you go.

This rosewood-effect dining table has been made out of MDF, a rubber graining roller and a deep-red vinyl silk paint.

HOW TO DO IT

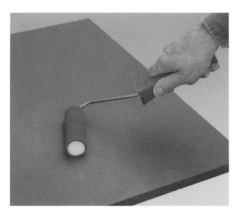

STEP 1 Paint the tabletop and edges with a coat of diluted PVA, 3 parts glue to 1 part water, to seal the surface.

STEP 2 Apply a coat of the red base colour and leave it to dry. Check for coverage and, if it needs one, apply a second base coat.

STEP 3 Mix up the glaze using 4 parts glaze to 1 part black paint.

STEP 4 Paint the glaze over the red base coat using a flat-ended paint brush. Gently wipe the cotton cloth over the wet surface so that only the thinnest layer of glaze remains. Don't scrub it all off, and leave a fine film of glaze for the graining.

STEP 6 Do the edges of the tabletop in exactly the same way. Leave the graining to dry and then apply two coats of clear matt varnish.

STEP 5 Hold the graining roller with both hands with the ridges curving down. Beginning at one end, hold the roller on the glazed surface and gently pull it towards you, rolling it over as you go. Having reached the extremity, begin rocking it back the other way, still pulling it towards you. Continue to the end and begin again alongside the first strip.

Sitting-dining room

The large room with a dining area at one end and the sitting area at the other has been around for a very long time. Large Victorian and Edwardian houses often featured tall folding doors between the reception rooms, to be opened up for large social gatherings. The open-plan lifestyle came in with the 1960s and, by the end of the 1970s, there were not many downstairs dividing walls left standing. For many years now new houses have been built to an open-plan design downstairs to make them feel as spacious as possible. Recent trends have seen the dining area become more defined, with low walls, glass bricks and screens being used to reinforce the fact that the room serves two different purposes.

Lighting is one way of subtly separating the eating from the seating areas. The sitting area needs relaxed lighting with table lamps or wall lights, while the dining table can be lit from above.

The seating and eating areas should ideally complement each other while being divided into separate areas. There are a number of ways to achieve this effect. Five areas you need to look at include:

Colour

When choosing the colour for the dining end of your room you must look at the room as a whole, which means taking all the existing colours into account. The furniture, curtains, carpets and paintings at one end must not look out of place with what you choose for the other. One of the projects in the following section shows how to use the same background colour throughout, and then mask off sections of wall and paint blocks of a deeper, more intense version of the same colour. This gives the dining area a different character while retaining a harmonious colour scheme. For a more dramatic effect, use the same technique but with blocks of contrasting colour.

Lighting

Clever lighting alone can define the different areas and make the same colour look warmer, cooler, brighter or more faded. The sitting area needs to have a relaxing atmosphere, which can be achieved with table lamps, wall lights and accent lights directed onto your favourite things. The dining table can be lit from above with a track of halogen spotlights, a chandelier or candelabra, depending upon the furniture style.

Flooring

One of the clearest ways of saying this end is for comfort and the other is for eating, is to have different types of flooring. This could be linoleum or a floating wooden floor at one end and a fitted carpet at the other. If this idea sounds too fixed, then consider fitting one type of flooring throughout and using a large round rug as the focus point in the sitting room.

Screening

A screen describes a barrier other than a wall – it could be solid and transparent, such as a glass brick wall, or something that you can see through, like cube shelving or a line of wooden rods. A semi-sheer curtain on a decorative rail (as shown in one of the following projects) is a good compromise because it can be drawn to section off the dining area for special occasions, and when drawn back softly frames both sides.

Furniture and accessories

Dining furniture for a dual-purpose room should be lighter and more compact than something for a dining room. Choose a square or circular table with extra flaps or panels so that it can expand when necessary and not be too obtrusive at other times. A sideboard is ideal in a room like this because the plates, glasses and cutlery can be hidden away conveniently close to the table. After years in the furniture wilderness, the sideboard is now an absolute 'must-have' in contemporary homes.

THE PROJECTS

The two projects on the following pages show subtle yet effective ways of separating the eating from the seating areas of a sitting-dining room. The first, a semi-sheer curtain divider, is the modern equivalent of Edwardian or Victorian folding doors between reception rooms. The second project shows how to use colour blocking to separate the two areas while keeping the same colour scheme throughout the room. Incorporate your personal style in the colours you choose.

Tables in sitting-dining rooms need to be lighter and more compact than those in separate dining rooms, so they are not too obtrusive over the whole area.

PROJECT ONE

Curtain divider

The treatment you choose for your sitting or dining room must reflect your own lifestyle. There is little point in having a semi-sheer curtain divider if you also own a large boisterous dog, no matter how much you like the idea! And avoid any fabric with too much bulk because the best curtains should hang as flat panels without any gathering. Embroidered sari fabric will give an exotic look while muslin is modern and minimalist, but you could also use a light cotton canvas as a flat 'wall' of colour.

This curtain divider will subtly divide the seating and eating areas in a sitting-dining room. The best materials to use are light, so they hang as flat panels without any gathering. Semi-sheer fabric, muslin, embroidered sari fabric or light, cotton canvas are all ideal.

HOW TO DO IT

STEP 1 Measure an equal distance from the dining end to the centre of the room on opposite walls, and mark these points on the skirting in pencil.

STEP 2 Use a line plumbed to the skirting board. Take a vertical measurement up to the ceiling height (using a straight edge with a spirit level) and make a pencil mark. Run a length of string across the ceiling between the two marks to be a guideline for the rail fitting.

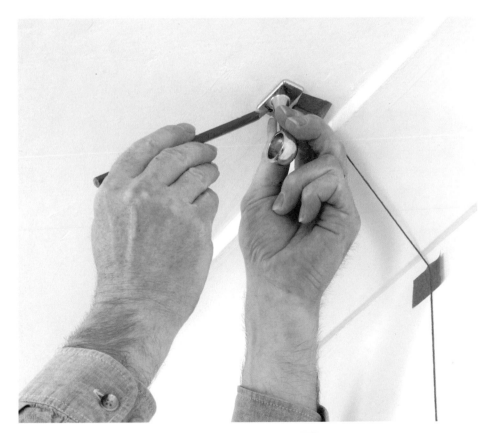

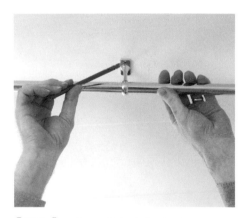

STEP 4 Drill out all the holes for the screws and slide the centre fixing onto the rail and screw in position.

STEP 5 Insert the cavity wall plugs. These are specially designed with claws to grip plasterboard from the back as the screws go in.

STEP 6 Clip the curtain rings onto the fabric or slip the curtain header tabs onto the rail.

STEP 3 Mark the positions for the screws to hold the rail fittings. The rails are supplied with fittings, usually one at each end with one in the middle.

YOU WILL NEED:

- DECORATOR'S
  MASKING TAPE
- PLUMB LINE
- STRAIGHT EDGE
- SET SQUARE
- PENCIL
- MATCH POTS
  (EMULSIONS,
  METALLICS OR
  TEXTURED PAINTS)
- PAINTBRUSH
- WALLPAPER PASTE IF
  COLOUR-WASHING

PROJECT TWO

Colour blocking

The wonderful thing about this decorating idea is that you can use sample pots for all the feature colours. The base colour is applied throughout the whole room, then the dining area is enlivened with blocks of colour. This can be done in all sorts of ways using different colours and textures. A multicoloured wall of squares, a graduated colour change from left to right, or deeper, more saturated shades of the background colour are some ideas to try. Contrasts in texture can also be introduced with metallic paints, chalky distempers or by thinning the emulsion paint with wallpaper paste to make a transparent glaze.

The wall of this dining area is decorated in multicoloured squares, but the colour scheme of the whole room is the same. You can introduce contrasts in texture by using metallic, chalky or glazed paint.

HOW TO DO IT

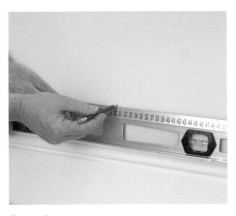

STEP 1 Having decided upon the shape, size and position of the squares on the wall, mark the verticals along the skirting board in pencil (for instance, 30 cm – 15 cm – 30 cm – 15 cm).

STEP 2 Hang the plumb line down the wall as a vertical guide, then use the straight edge and a pencil to make guide marks for the same grid going up the wall (30 cm – 15 cm – 30 cm – 15cm).

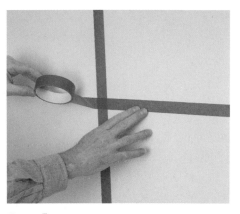

STEP 3 Run tape up from the skirting board in straight lines. Then, using the level to check that the corners are square, run tape horizontally across the wall, intersecting the verticals and completing the grid of squares.

STEP 4 For a colour-wash effect mix wallpaper paste into emulsion (half and half) and spread the glaze with random brush strokes.

STEP 5 Apply the colour of your choice in all the large squares.

STEP 6 Once the paint has dried, carefully peel off all the masking tape.

TIP
• You can use metallic paints as well, to catch the light and make the room appear larger. These are now generally available from DIY stores everywhere.

Bedrooms

The bedroom should be a sanctuary, a place of rest, a temple of calm. But since it is also the room least on display to friends, it is easy to pay less attention to bedrooms than to other rooms. The bedroom has a range of practical functions which need to be taken into account in any redesign. Apart from sleeping, it is a place for storing clothes, getting dressed, styling hair, reading and perhaps watching television. Children's rooms have another set of functions that need to be taken into account, not least their own preferences. Above all, the fact that bedrooms are the most private rooms in the house means they are the perfect place to express yourself.

Traditional bedroom

Traditional style in the bedroom means grand, comfortable and irresistible but certainly not old-fashioned in any way. This is the sort of room where you should feel very grown up and since it is also where you do most of your dreaming, it should be the room of your dreams. The star of the show is the bed, which should be as comfortable as your budget allows, with a good bed head, a bedside table for your champagne or morning cup of tea, soft but effective lighting and twice as many pillows as you really need.

Alcoves are ideal places for shelving, and to position dressing tables and mirrors. Look out for traditional furniture in local furniture auctions.

This style uses lots of traditional ideas – it could be very feminine, with lace, frills and satin, or have the understated elegance of dark wooden furniture, monogrammed cotton pillowcases, satin-edged blankets and a cream woven coverlet. And how about a four-poster bed with a plump eiderdown or a shiny brass bed with a patchwork quilt? As this is the one room in your house that people visit by invitation only, you can truly please yourself.

A low-ceilinged room would look smaller with a four-poster, but a similar lighter effect can be achieved by fixing curtain rails above the bed hung with muslin or voile drapes. If the idea of being curtained in sounds too claustrophobic, then a canopy on the wall behind the bed head with fabric drapes falling to the floor will frame the bed, giving a romantic but less enclosed look. The canopy can be fixed to something as simple as a wooden shelf fitted with a decorative moulding.

You can really work wonders with fabric and a staple gun. Any existing headboard can be revamped with a new fabric cover, and a plain bed can be dressed up with a headboard of MDF covered with upholstery foam and fabric, which is then screwed onto the wall or hung from a curtain pole. Trimmings of fringe, tassels, buttons, ribbons, lace or fancy braids can be stitched on or attached with a glue gun.

Storage

Unless there is space for a separate dressing room you will need a wardrobe and drawers for clothes, somewhere for shoes and perhaps a dressing table. Make use of any alcoves for shelving or hanging space and, if you have a bay window, fit a built-in window seat with lift-off lids covered with cushions to match the bedcover or curtain fabric, and storage space below. If wardrobes are fitted make sure that they suit the look of the bedroom. Wooden door panels can be removed and replaced with soft panels of gathered fabric on net curtain wires. Visit local furniture auctions where you can often find traditional bedroom suites. They really don't make furniture the way they used to, except at the top end of the market, but old wooden furniture given a new paint finish and upholstery can look fantastic, and will cost much less than similar new furniture in traditional styles.

Try a stripped pine blanket chest to store out-of-season clothes or, if you've had enough of pine, give it a dark stain or try something like découpage or a crackle glazed effect. Boxes on castors under the bed are a good place to keep your shoes. But remember that all storage for items currently in use should be easily accessible otherwise it just doesn't work. If there isn't enough floor space to pull out an underbed drawer, then keep the drawer for things that you won't need for a while.

Walls and floors

Choose colours that are easy on the eye and patterns that won't keep you awake at night. Don't try to match everything or the result could be a bedroom with no personality. Stripes, checks and floral patterns can all be combined if the colours are similar, as can different textures like tweed, cotton, velvet and linen. Don't use too many different colours though, two or three main ones are enough with accents of contrasting colours in small amounts. Fabric trimmed with a ribbon border can be used on the walls in place of wallpaper, or hung from a picture rail around the bed. Pattern motifs can also be copied from textiles and made into stencils to decorate the walls or furniture. Floors should ideally be soft carpets, but if you prefer wooden floorboards, make sure you have 'islands' of soft bedside rugs.

Windows

A traditional bedroom has curtains. Indulge in generous drapes, deep pelmets and black-out linings. Generosity is the key, and it is better to use lots of cheap fabric like unbleached calico or suit lining, and dress it up with a boldly contrasting ribbon or deep fringe border than to use small amounts of an expensive fabric.

Accessories and lighting

Have at least one good mirror on the wall and for a real touch of luxury, nothing beats a vase of fresh flowers. Think about the practical lighting you need for wardrobes and drawers as well as pretty bedside lighting – if you have an overhead light use a dimmer switch for a shadowy, sensual atmosphere.

Decluttering

Most of the clutter in the bedroom comes from newspapers, books, shoes, laundry (clean and dirty), make up, accessories and jewellery. It helps if you begin by having a place for everything, then all you have to do is keep up the good work. New stuff arrives all the time, so unless you constantly chuck out the unwanted, things will begin to pile up.

Small cupboards

Give a small cupboard a traditional French country look by painting it green, blue or deep pink and replace its door panels with chicken wire sprayed to match. Stretch net curtain wires above and below the panels on the back of the doors with screw-in eyelets, and gather fabric panels on to them. Choose a fabric that you already have in the room.

THE PROJECTS
The following projects show how to transform your bedroom into the traditional style using both decorative and functional ways. Some accessories and trimmings should do the rest.

A canopy fixed to the wall behind the bed head with drapes falling either side frames the bed in a romantic look that is less enclosed than the four-poster.

YOU WILL NEED:

- **STENCIL CARD**
- **TRACING PAPER**
- **CRAFT KNIFE**
- **CUTTING MAT OR PIECE OF THICK CARD**
- **SPRAYMOUNT**
- **STENCIL BRUSH**
- **RULER**
- **PLUMB LINE AND BLUETACK**
- **MATCHPOTS OR STENCIL PAINT**
- **PLATE**

PROJECT ONE

Stencilling a wall

Stencilling has been around for a very long time but not everyone has the confidence to cut out a stencil and paint their bedroom wall. This little stencil motif will get you started but be warned, once you realise how easy and effective stencilling can be you won't want to stop! Stencils can be cut from any waxed cardboard or plastic specially formulated for this purpose. The advantage of plastic is that it is transparent and easier to align, but with a simple pattern like this one you can draw a vertical line through it, and visually line it up with a plumb line each time you move it. The pattern is stencilled with a half-drop on each second row.

This simple stencil motif is easy to paint and very effective on a traditional bedroom wall. Choose the stencil paint in your favourite calm colour.

HOW TO DO IT

STEP 1 Photocopy or trace the pattern and spray the back of it with Spraymount. Stick It onto the stencil material. Place the stencil material on the cutting mat, and cut out the shape using a craft knife. Peel off the paper and draw a line through the middle as a guide.

STEP 2 Spray the back of the stencil with Spraymount. This will make the stencil sticky enough to stay flat against the wall, and stop the paint from bleeding under the stencil. It will also peel off the wall leaving no residue.

STEP 3 Put some paint onto the plate and load up the stencil brush with paint. Now wipe most of the paint off on a sheet of kitchen paper (you only need a tiny bit of paint for stencilling).

STEP 5 Move the plumb line across and begin the second row 30 cm across from the first, but start this one 15 cm from the top of the wall. Stencil the next motif 30 cm below and continue in the same way as before. The third row is started 30 cm from the top, and the following one 15 cm, and so on.

Enlarge the stencil below and transfer onto plastic or stencil paper. Line up the stencils on the wall as shown in the second sketch below.

STEP 4 The first line of stencil pattern is applied in a straight line 30 cm apart. Starting in one corner, fix the plumb line to the top of the wall, measure 30 cm across and down, and line up the top of the stencil. Check the centre line with the plumb line, then apply the paint in a light swirling stroke. Begin at the edges and work inwards. Don't overdo it as you can always return to add more paint once it is dry. Complete the first row.

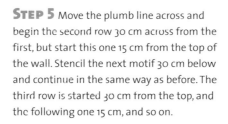

PROJECT TWO

The four poster

This project shows you how to build a four-poster frame around a plain bed, and once the frame is in place you can choose a fabric to give the bed the look of your choice – floral chintz for an English country house style, or calico and gingham for an American folk look.

The first key step is to decide the height of your bed, which should relate to the ceiling height in your bedroom, and then follow the simple construction steps. The frame can be painted or varnished depending upon the style of your room.

A four-poster frame transforms a bed into the ultimate in romantic decadence. The choice of fabric will give the bed its look – whether it's floral chintz, calico and gingham, or sheer white muslin.

HOW TO DO IT

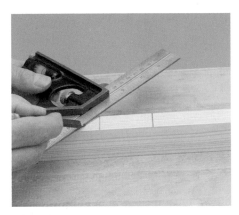

STEP 1 Measure the length of the bed base and add 10 cm to allow for the width of the uprights. Mitre the top and lower side lengths to this measurement. Measure the width of the bed base, and mitre the top and lower end pieces to this measurement. Sandpaper all the cut edges.

STEP 2 The top ends and sides are fitted flush with the top of the uprights. To find the height for the broad lower planks surrounding the bed, measure the distance from the floor to halfway up the mattress. This is where the top of the lower planks should be fixed to the uprights.

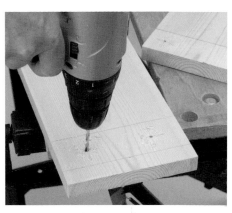

STEP 3 Make up the bed ends first. Lay down parallel one set of uprights, with the top and lower end lengths between them. Drill holes for two screws at each joint. Apply wood glue and screw the pieces together. Repeat to make up the other bed end.

STEP 4 Drill and countersink screw holes in all the top and lower side pieces, and pilot holes in the uprights, making sure that these screws will miss the ones already located there.

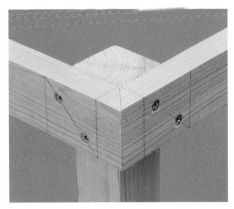

STEP 5 The top sides can now be screwed in place, with your assistant supporting one end while you stand on a stepladder and secure the other. The completed bed frame can be painted, stained or varnished, and hung with tab-top curtains.

STEP 6 This is where you need an assistant – ask a friend for help or prop one frame end against the wall with the bed pushed against it. Support the lower sides at the foot end while screwing them to the uprights at the head end. Have your assistant hold the foot end upright while you screw the lower sides to it.

TIP
• If you prefer a more gathered curtain effect, fit a standard curtain rail to the inside edge of the top frame and hang the curtains from it in the usual way.

YOU WILL NEED:

• SMALL TABLE – THE
  EDGE NEEDS A
  DEPTH OF 25 MM
  FOR THE VELCRO,
  IF NOT THEN FIX ON
  A HARDBOARD
  STRIP EDGE

• FABRIC FOR THE
  DRESSING TABLE
  SKIRT

• SELF-ADHESIVE
  VELCRO TO FIT
  AROUND THE FRONT
  AND SIDES OF THE
  TABLE TOP

• TRIMMING FOR THE
  TOP EDGE (OPTIONAL)

• SHEET OF
  TOUGHENED TABLE-
  TOP GLASS WITH
  SMOOTH EDGES

• SEWING MACHINE
  AND THREAD, OR
  IRON-ON HEMMING
  TAPE AND AN IRON

PROJECT THREE

Dressing table with storage space below

A plain table with a shelf below can be easily converted into a dressing table and storage area with the help of fabric, Velcro, a sheet of glass and a free-standing mirror. Once you've made the floor-length fabric skirt for the table, add lace, ribbon or braid edging and top it with a sheet of toughened, smooth-edged glass ordered to size from your local glazier.

A plain table with a shelf beneath can be easily transformed into a traditional dressing table, with useful storage for the less attractive cosmetic bottles and tubes you'd rather not have on display.

HOW TO DO IT

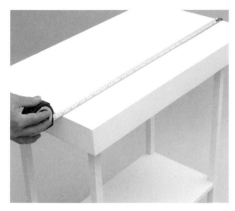

STEP 1 Measure the height from the table top to the floor, and then measure around the sides and the front, adding a bit extra for an overlap. If you want to pleat the 'skirt', then allow more fabric. Divide the length into two.

STEP 2 Depending upon the condition of the table top, either cover it with fabric or a lace cloth, or paint or stain it with the colour of your choice.

STEP 3 Stick the looped side of the Velcro around the table edge.

STEP 4 Turn back a hem on the top and bottom of the skirt, and sew or bond with iron-on tape.

STEP 5 Sew or stick the other side of the Velcro tape to the top hem of the fabric. Press the skirt onto the table edge. Have one piece overlap the other by about 20 mm where they meet in the middle. Fix a small square of looped Velcro to fasten the overlap. And finally, place the glass on the table top. Add a vase of flowers and a mirror and hide all your undesirables behind the curtain!

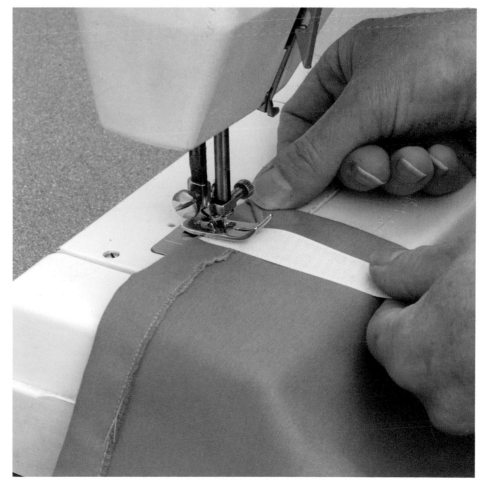

Contemporary bedroom

There are many different ways to create a contemporary look, but the style is predominantly about clean lines, clear space and creating an atmosphere. This is the age of the senses, where aromatherapy and feng shui are considered mainstream, and natural colours, fabrics and decorating materials are understood to bring a feeling of well-being. Minimalism has been the biggest recent influence on home decorating, and the quickest way to get the contemporary look is to clear the surfaces, put away all your clutter, lay a wooden floor and light some candles.

Efficient storage is a must in the contemporary bedroom. It is the only way to keep clothes, shoes, cosmetics and jewellery out of sight and maintain the minimalist style. Ideally, clothes would be stored in a separate dressing room, freeing up the bedroom space of functional furniture, but in reality few of us have this choice, so we have to be creative with our storage options. Five key things to consider when creating a contemporary bedroom include...

Ideally, the only furniture in a contemporary bedroom is the bed. Walk-in wardrobes or separate dressing rooms are an effective luxury which keep the bedroom clutter-free.

Furniture

The double bed is a very big piece of furniture which will immediately dominate the room. If you give the bed a contemporary makeover then the rest of the room can follow. If you already have a good bed then it is worth keeping because they are very expensive. Give it a change of style by adding a drop-in headboard, which is one of the projects in this section.

Pine bed heads with turned spindles were so popular but now look very dated. They can be boxed in with sheets of MDF or plywood, and painted or covered with foam and fabric to make a really comfortable back rest. Basic upholstery like this can be tackled with a staple gun, double-sided tape and a glue gun. Stick the foam to the MDF, staple the fabric over the top of it and neaten the edges with a plain ribbon trimming stuck on with the hot glue gun. You can do it!

An alternative plain and minimal style is the Japanese look. If your budget is tight, and you don't mind sleeping on a futon, then you can make a really cheap and stylish bed base out of a pair of wooden pallets. The wood will need sanding to get rid of potential splinters and then you just put the futon on top. Keep bedside tables low, place woven grass mats on each side of the bed, fit paper shades and blinds, and hang framed Japanese prints on the walls.

If you are starting from scratch then go for a low-level platform bed with built-in storage below and reading lights in the headboard. There are some amazing new wooden beds around that have a wardrobe's worth of drawers built in, but be warned because they are very expensive. Iron bed frames are cool and popular, and there are loads of original designs made by small companies. Look for individual makers in magazine small ads if you are looking for something unique. They are also made in different finishes, aluminium being one of the latest styles, and all the big furniture stores have their own ranges of metal beds. If you choose one be sure to have plenty of pillows because they are cold and hard to lean against.

The Shaker style is now making a comeback, even though it's over 250 years since it first appeared in America (the Shakers were an offshoot of the Quakers). The Shakers lived in community houses without any unnecessary decoration or personal possessions, keeping the floor space clear and putting everything away in built-in cupboards. All of these ideas strike a minimalist chord, and the furniture is so beautiful that the reproduction Shaker style is now one of the most popular styles around.

Wardrobes and chests of drawers are large enough to ruin any sense of space you create with careful use of lighting and colour, so think carefully whether you really need them. If you only have skirts, shirts and trousers to hang up then fit a double rail in a small wardrobe and use the full height of it. Space below hanging clothes can so easily become untidy, so put in a shoe rack or storage boxes. Also check out new wardrobes with frosted glass doors, but be aware that they will only look good if everything inside is tidy.

If you are lucky enough to have a big room, think about having a false wall built to make a

You can't go wrong with white as a colour scheme – it reflects the light, is flattering to the complexion and goes with everything. Off-whites look particularly good with wood.

If you've got windows to flaunt, make the most of them by fitting blinds into the window recesses or make them more dramatic with floor-to-ceiling billowing muslin drops.

walk-in wardrobe. This need not use up more than 1 m of room space (including the partition wall). This storage space is just right for all your clothes and shoes, suitcases and spare bedding. The only furniture needed in the bedroom would be the bed. Now that is luxury!

The way you decorate the bedroom windows depends on several things. Do you need to keep out draughts or traffic noise? Does the sun shine too brightly in the morning? Are the window frames attractive and do you have a nice view? Try thick curtains for absorbing noise and blocking draughts, making the room a lot more cosy. For a warm contemporary style use blankets, felt or lined fleece to make curtains. Block out the sun with black-out lining material, which costs a bit more than ordinary lining, but really is effective. If the window frames are a good feature, like the old wooden sash kind, they shouldn't be hidden away, and you can fit blinds into the window recess. There are some fabulous new materials and designs, including felt and denim for warmth, voile to allow the light in, pierced patterns and lots of variations on the classic Venetian blind.

Colour schemes

Bedroom colour schemes need to create a mood. A natural palette of greens, browns and off-whites look fabulous with wood. It is a sophisticated choice and these colours are also harmonious and relaxing. If you feel a bit wilder there are some wonderful rich colours to choose from. Bedroom colours can also be toned down or livened up for a change of mood by using the right lighting. Lilac, turquoise and pink are a wonderfully feminine combination with a contemporary edge, while cinnamon, oatmeal, mushroom and chocolate brown are warm, rich, masculine colours. Blue is spacious and dreamy, and white reflects the light, flatters the complexion and goes with virtually everything.

Lighting

Bedroom lighting can be divided into three definite areas. The room as a whole might need a large, central chandelier-type light fitted with a dimmer switch. The bedside area needs reading lights, while task lighting will help you find things in the wardrobe after dark. Choose lights that switch on when you open the door, or simple, battery-powered lights for occasional use.

Flooring

The flooring for the contemporary bedroom is best kept plain. If you have wooden floorboards paint them with wood wash that is a lighter version of one of the colours used in the room. Pale wooden floors look good, and soft rugs can be used by the bedside to warm your toes in the morning.

Decorating this room is really very personal. It's a place to enjoy being wrapped in those colours, textures and patterns that please you. And whatever you do, never sacrifice comfort for style in the bedroom.

Decluttering

Clutter can be everything. It's the mail that arrives in the morning that sits next to the tea things by the nail varnish and the hair slides, with the case for your glasses and the pen by the notepad right next to the phone. And sometimes it threatens to engulf us. When this point is reached it is time for some serious decluttering.

Try to clear the morning clutter when you leave the bedroom. Have a deep-sided tray for the morning tea or coffee and make sure that the post, newspapers and glasses from the night before are taken out there and then. Look out for a stylish bed tray or breakfast tray – they have two side compartments that act as legs with a sturdy section across the middle. A bedside magazine rack is a necessity, and once you have one you may wonder why they are not considered standard bedroom accessories. Also buy matching boxes in a range

of sizes – choose leather, wicker, clear Perspex or canvas. Mount bookshelves on the wall in an alcove or as a series of modular cube shelving units. Keep videos in a box with a lid because even if they are neatly stacked their packaging still looks like clutter. Buy a wooden ladder to lean up against the wall – use a dark wood stain to smarten it up and use it as a temporary resting place for discarded clothes and towels. Buy a laundry bin and waste paper bin to match the room style and finally an open shoe rack big enough for the shoes you wear all the time, keeping out-of-season and special occasion pairs stacked in matching shoe boxes. Decluttering is all about learning to be organised and stylish at the same time.

The natural colours of wood and the stone flooring, with the clean, clutter-free lines of built-in wardrobes give this bedroom a contemporary look.

THE PROJECTS
The two projects on the following pages suggest how to start achieving a contemporary look in your own bedroom. A fresh coat of paint, some flexible lighting and some disciplined decluttering should do the rest.

YOU WILL NEED
- WOOD AS FOLLOWS:
  1 BACK 18-MM MDF,
  1 SHEET OF 2.4 M X
  1.2 M;
  1 TOP SHELF PAR SOFT
  WOOD, 14.5 CM X
  2.5 M;
  2 SIDES 18-MM MDF,
  1.2 M X 61 CM (SEE
  PLAN FOR CUT-OUT);
  2 INNER SIDES 18-MM
  MDF, 48 CM X
  60 CM;
  2 SHELVES 18-MM
  MDF, 48 CM X 43 CM;
  2 TOPS 18 MM MDF,
  48 CM X 50 CM
- BOX OF TWIN-
  THREAD 50-MM No.
  6 SCREWS
- WOOD GLUE
- WOOD FILLER
- SANDPAPER
- PRIMER AND SATIN
  FINISH PAINT
- DRILL WITH
  COUNTERSINK, AND
  2-MM PILOT HOLE BIT
  AND SCREWDRIVER
  BIT
- LONG RULE
- COMBINATION
  SQUARE
- PENCIL
- TAPE MEASURE
- SMALL FOAM ROLLER
  AND TRAY

PROJECT ONE

A drop-in bed surround

Building a box headboard with a shelf and two side tables sounds ambitious but be assured, it is totally simple and the construction method is quite straightforward. It can be done with the most basic tool kit and it will make the bedroom look utterly chic.

The list on the left gives the sizes of all the pieces of MDF and softwood needed to make this surround to fit a 1.5 metre-wide double bed. Most timber merchants will cut the wood to size for a small fee, which will save time considering the number of different lengths needed.

This stunning bed surround is practical as well as chic. It can be an effective way of boxing in the now-dated pine bedheads, and you can either leave the surrounds painted or attach basic upholstery.

HOW TO DO IT

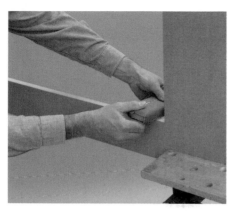

STEP 1 Cut out the waste from the two ends and sand the edges.

STEP 2 Draw positional guides for the assembly of the sides, back and inner sides. Mark these very carefully with pencil lines.

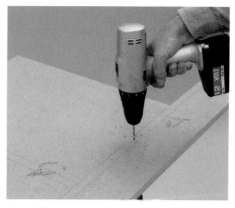

STEP 3 Drill pilot holes for the screws and countersink them.

STEP 4 Screw the sides and inner shelves to the back.

STEP 5 Add the shelves and the tops.

STEP 6 Fill and sand the countersink holes. Seal, prime and paint.

> **TIP**
> • Unpainted MDF looks good varnished. If you don't intend to paint it then use brass screws with screw-cup washers rather than countersunk screws. They will be a visible feature and look better than patches of woodfiller.

Use this sketch to help you position the surround correctly around your bed. You will need an assistant to help you drop it in place against the wall.

YOU WILL NEED:
- 2 M CORDUROY FABRIC
- 1.5 M ARTIFICIAL FUR FABRIC
- 1.5 M OF 125 g QUILT WADDING
- PINS
- THREAD
- SEWING MACHINE

PROJECT TWO

Using textures to create a comfort zone

Most of the time we spend in the bedroom is in darkness, and this makes it perfect for exploring the use of different textures. These must change with the seasons if they are to be fully appreciated. Imagine stepping out of bed on a hot summer night onto cool woven grass matting or onto a thin sheepskin fleece in winter. The summer bedroom should be airy, with billowing muslin at the windows and cool cotton sheets on the bed. In winter the bed is more of a cosy nest, with knitted hot water-bottle covers, soft velvet cushions, thick blankets and flannel sheets. This bed cover, which is 50 per cent throw and 50 per cent quilt, combines two contrasting textures, corduroy and fake fur, to give 100 per cent comfort! Choose a wonderfully soft and warm fabric such as artificial fur, fleece or the more hard-wearing corduroy.

This bed cover combines fake fur on one side with corduroy on the other, each sandwiching quilt wadding, to create the ultimate winter warmer.

HOW TO DO IT

STEP 1 Lay the corduroy on a flat surface with the wadding and fur fabric placed on the top. Place the two top fabrics 50 mm inside the top edge and on one side edge of the cord.

STEP 2 Trim away the fur on the other two sides to make a 50 mm border all round.

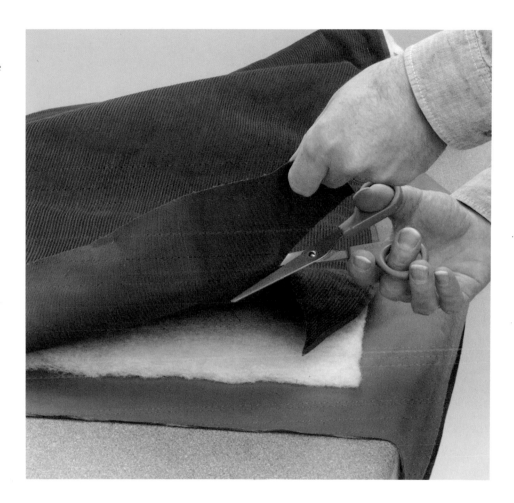

STEP 3 Mitre the corners. When you fold them over the two edges meet to make a neat finish.

STEP 4 Fold the fur border over and pin it to the cord. Set the sewing machine to satin stitch, and sew all around the edge and up the middle of the mitres so that all the cut edges are sealed and sewn.

TIP
• The choice of feature fabric is up to you, it could be velvet, corduroy, brushed cotton or even a knitted blanket. Check that the textures will be good companions when you choose them.

Teenage boy's room

Forget about the stereotypical messy teenage boy, he's an urban myth. Boys want to live in nice surroundings just as much as girls do. They have strong ideas about colour, fashion and relaxation and will not thank you for making these decisions for them. Good TV decorating programmes appeal to young people's imaginations, especially with their rule-breaking ideas. It may seem like a contradiction, but being seen as an individual matters just as much to a teenager as being in fashion. And who wants to do things the traditional way when you can get the same effect with panel adhesive in a fraction of the time? Unfortunately what goes up will probably need to come down at some time, and this is where screws have the advantage over glues.

Get teenagers involved in any redecorating from the start. They'll have strong ideas about the colours and style they want, and you might even get them to help...

Start the project with a conference. Decorating influences can come from all over the place – sport, music, fashion and films are the four most obvious ones and a good starting point. One way to do something original and fashionable is to mix ideas and decorate using the key features of recognisable brands of clothing. Think trainers, skateboard, surfing, snowboard and other sports gear with a distinctive style and you'll be on the right track. If he is into surfing make a stencil of the logo on his surfboard. It doesn't have to be too literal, just the colours of a brand will be enough to make the statement.

So far it's easy but the difficulty lies in keeping his enthusiasm alive during the boring preparatory stages. It is hard to be too enthusiastic about primers, undercoats and filling so you may have to resort to a good old-fashioned bribe. Try offering a coveted CD to listen to while working, or a new duvet cover, a cool bedside light or a full-length mirror when the room is finished.

Colour can affect moods, so try and talk him out of black walls because they are seriously depressing. And the advantage of another colour is that it can always be painted over (unlike black). Just go with the flow! If the room is small it's a good idea to paint the furniture the same colour as the walls, and this is a good way to update wardrobes and chests of drawers that have been around for a while. Whatever the room's dimensions he will want to have friends stay over. A sofa-bed is ideal but alternatives include a bed in a bag, a rolled-up camping mat that doubles as a bolster, or a foam cube that unfolds to become a single mattress. A sleeping bag rolled up and tied with a belt makes a pretty good cushion too.

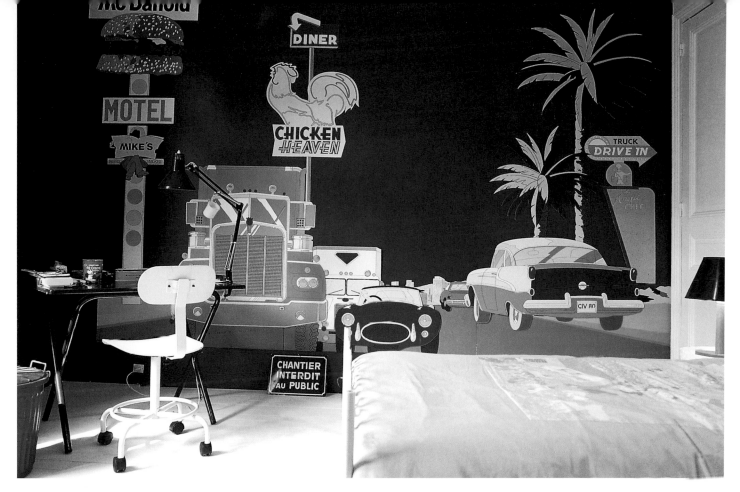

Homework area

If the room is going to be used for schoolwork it is important to make it easy for him to study. We all work in different ways but an organised work area is always helpful. Even if he reads the books sprawled out on the floor, it is better if they are kept on a shelf rather than under the bed. And either buy a desk or build a work table with shelving and a good light source. Make it big enough for a computer, television and stereo as well, then buy him a swivel chair and he can really get down to business.

There is one more thing that every teenager needs, regardless of his or her interests, and that is a huge noticeboard – kill two birds with one stone by covering a wall or all the walls with softboard. This is the material used to line school corridors so that work can be pinned up. It can be painted to look like any other wall, and used to display anything and everything. It is also great at noise reduction. It should be compulsory!

When it comes to flooring it is best to choose something that won't stain but will be as soundproof as possible. A good underlay will block out most of the beat from his stereo, and carpet tiles are good because they can be lifted and replaced if damage occurs. Hardboard is cheap and under-used as a flooring material. It can be laid in large sheets fixed down with lines of domed upholstery studs, and painted with floor paint to give a hard-edged industrial look. And if the floor is hard, make sure he also has a big soft rug to laze about on – because that's what he'll like best.

> ### THE PROJECTS
> The two projects on the following pages give street cred to functional bedroom furniture. The first project shows how to make a bedhead out of scaffold poles, while the second adds a hip-hop stencil to transform a cheap desk.

American culture is a firm favourite among teenagers, and if you're going to take on America, like this floor-to-ceiling mural, you've got to think big!

YOU WILL NEED:

- 6 LENGTHS OF
  SCAFFOLD POLE CUT
  TO THE FOLLOWING
  LENGTHS:
  4 LENGTHS OF 50 CM
  FOR THE UPRIGHTS;
  2 LENGTHS OF 1 M FOR
  THE CROSS-PIECES
- 2 ELBOW FITTINGS
- 2 T FITTINGS
- 2 END SOCKETS
- ALLEN KEY (USED FOR
  TIGHTENING METAL
  JOINTS)
- 2.5 M OF 91 CM WIDE
  MEDIUM- TO
  HEAVYWEIGHT
  COTTON DUCK
  (COARSE COTTON
  OR LINEN)
- SEWING MACHINE
- THREAD
- SEWING MACHINE
  NEEDLE FOR SEWING
  DENIM

This industrial bed
head is made out of
scaffold poles, with a
section of denim for a
back rest. This heavy
bedhead will need
screwing into the
floor due to its
weight, so make sure
you are able to do this
before you start.

PROJECT ONE

The scaffold pole bed head

This project takes the building site into the bedroom by using scaffold poles to make a bed head. You can also make a hanging rail in a similar way. There are companies who specialise in scaffold beds and platforms, but this project uses galvanised scaffold materials, bought from a builder's merchant, to make a serious, industrial-chic statement. A piece of coarse cotton or linen make a comfortable back rest. The items in the list on the left are for a single bed.

HOW TO DO IT

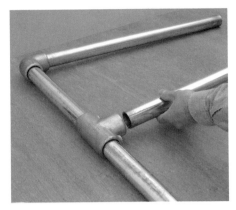

STEP 1 Slot the elbow fittings on to the end of one of the cross-pieces and add two 50-cm uprights. Fit the T fittings on to the other cross-piece and fit it on to the uprights. Don't tighten anything up yet.

STEP 2 Wrap the fabric around the two cross-pieces and mark the position for a joining seam at the back with chalk.

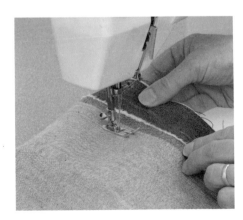

STEP 3 Fold the seam over at the back and sew it flat with a double row of stitching.

STEP 4 Loosen the joints at one side and slip the fabric over the two cross-pieces. Tighten up the fittings with the Allen key.

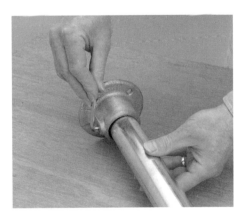

STEP 5 Complete the bed head by adding the two lower poles and the end fittings.

STEP 6 As this is a very heavy bed head it has to be well secured. Fit the poles into two endplates and screw them to the floor using large screws. And do check that there no water pipes passing underneath the fixing points!

YOU WILL NEED:
- 1 PLAIN AND VERY CHEAP DESK (SECOND-HAND IS BEST)
- 1 LARGE CAN OF ALUMINIUM PAINT, PLUS SMALL CANS OF OTHER COLOURS (YOU WILL NEED TWO COLOURS FOR EACH NUMBER STENCIL THAT YOU CHOOSE)
- STENCIL CARD
- PENCIL
- SCALPEL
- MASKING TAPE
- SPRAYMOUNT

PROJECT TWO

Customising a cheap computer desk in the hip-hop style

Everyone needs somewhere to work but that doesn't mean it has to look boring and worthy. This project takes a really cheap, white-laminated, fibreboard desk and gives it street cred. The numerals could be exchanged for letters done in the same shadowed style, and whatever pattern you choose, remember it doesn't matter if it's slightly off-centre or if the spray drifts a bit at the edges – it'll still look good.

A basket-ball style stencil has transformed this cheap, white, fibreboard desk. Add stickers, labels and logos to complete the look.

HOW TO DO IT

STEP 1 Take a photocopy from a favourite sports sweatshirt.

STEP 2 Enlarge the numerals to about 30 cm in length and transfer the patterns onto the stencil card. Cut out two stencils. One should just be the letter outline, the other should have stencil bridges added on letters such as Os and Rs to keep the shape intact.

STEP 3 Use a scalpel to cut out the stencils. Spray the back with Spraymount. One stencil is for the main motif, the other for the border.

STEP 4 Protect a well-ventilated area with lots of newspaper and then roller or brush the aluminium paint onto the desk.

STEP 5 Attach the first stencil to the desk with masking tape. Spray this with your first chosen colour.

STEP 6 Spray through the second stencil in the second colour to create the border. Repeat this as many times as you like on the top, the outsides and insides and then add as many stickers, logos and labels as you like.

Teenage girl's room

Decorating is influenced by changes in fashion, and never more so than in a teenage girl's room. The big problem is that fashion is an industry and in order to keep it ticking over looks have to change with the seasons. What is totally 'in' now might be totally 'out' in six months' time. Do not despair though, there are a few hardy perennials that manage to stay cool throughout and denim tops the chart. The blue denim theme runs through all the projects in this section, but apart from the cushion cover made from old jeans the same methods could be used to suit different fabrics.

Plan any bedroom make-over together and make sure she gets to choose the style. If you absolutely hate the combinations she chooses, you could always try reverse psychology and pretend it was exactly what you were thinking for the room too...

If this is the first major make-over since childhood, take time to plan the decorating together. If you're stuck for inspiration then watch TV decorating programmes and look through magazines, colour charts and fabric samples. Leaving the toys and other childhood paraphernalia behind is a big step in a girl's life. It can be a bit much if everything familiar and comforting is suddenly whisked away before you're ready to say goodbye so, whatever you do, don't make big changes when she's not there.

A teenager's bedroom is much more than somewhere to sleep. It is a room to entertain friends, experiment with clothes and make-up, listen to music and study. Planned well, it can be all these things and more. A good way of planning room space is to cut out paper versions of all the furniture and move it around on a room plan. Do this to scale using squared paper and draw in all the fixed features, like radiators, windows, doors, chimney breasts, alcoves and any built-in wardrobes or shelves. If the room is small, a platform bed with a desk underneath may be ideal. These used to be too rickety for older children but they are now being made in stronger materials . They are a brilliant solution if space is limited because all the sleep and study space is fitted into a compact area, and the rest of the room can be geared towards leisure

Dressing table

A dressing table is not strictly necessary, but will be appreciated. There is no point in denying it, most girls need somewhere to keep a lot of nail polish, make-up and hair-styling equipment. They also need mirrors – a long one to see the whole picture and a small one for close-ups. She will be the envy of all her friends if you wall-mount a mirror surrounded by light bulbs in the film star's dressing-room style – use low watt, soft-glow type bulbs.

Clothes will pile up on anything that stands still, and a small clothes rail on castors is a really good idea even if there is a perfectly good wardrobe in the room. This is more like the rail a model would have backstage with a selection of outfits for the catwalk. Encourage her to keep her school clothes on the rail at night instead of on the floor and to keep other clothes on the rail or in the wardrobe the rest of the time.

If, like most teenage girls, she likes to dance, you could divide the floor space in two and having carpet in one half and laminated wooden floorboards in the other. This only works in a medium to large room, and a small room would look bigger and better with a laminated floor and rugs. If there is going to be music and dancing don't scrimp on the underlay – whatever flooring you choose this will act as soundproofing.

Colour

Wall colours are a personal choice, and the best thing is to step back and only offer your opinion if you're asked for it. If you absolutely hate the combinations she chooses then you could try reverse psychology and pretend that it's exactly what you had in mind for the dining room! If that doesn't cause an instant rethink, bear in mind that in the end it's only paint, and mistakes can always be put right with a coat of something less alarming.

The style of window treatment will very much depend on the overall look of the room – if she likes the ethnic look then something floaty like sari fabric would be lovely. A trip to a market is always fun and they are often a good place to buy ethnic accessories like lamps, cushions and throws. If she prefers a more contemporary cool look then blinds are the best bet. If you don't live near any trendy furniture stores, blinds can be bought by mail order and come in a wide range of materials, including denim and felt.

A new set of bed linen also works wonders and she'll be spoilt for choice. There are colours and patterns to suit every style and mood, so be adventurous and investigate all the possibilities before making a decision.

Storage

Storage is far less of a nightmare than it used to be because there are so many good systems on the market. They range from matching boxes to take everything from CDs to shoes, to modular storage cubes that can be added to if you need more space, to wire basket wardrobe organisers with stacks of drawers on castors. Send for all the catalogues (we have a list at the back of the book) then set yourselves a budget and take your pick. Shelves are always a good idea, and a high shelf on one wall makes a good retirement home for all those cuddly toys from childhood.

Lamps

Lamps are now fashionable accessories, having crossed over from furniture stores to gift shops. They are sold alongside novelty greetings cards, cushions and candles. Young consumers are well aware of the latest trends, and a wacky bedside lamp is rated as a top birthday or Christmas present. On a more practical level, think about getting an angle-poise lamp for studying and a wardrobe light. Finally, when all the hard work is done and the room looks out of this world, step back and let her take the credit for everything. It will be worth it!

THE PROJECTS
The two projects on the following pages both focus on denim, the fabric that refuses to date, and the ultimate in cool.

Alcoves can make interesting spaces for wall-mounted desks and bookshelves, keeping the homework side of the room to a compact corner.

YOU WILL NEED:

- DENIM – MEASURE THE WINDOW AREA AND THEN ADD HALF THE AREA AGAIN, PLUS A 20 MM SEAM ALLOWANCE TO ALL EDGES. NOTE THAT DENIM COMES IN DIFFERENT WIDTHS AND WEIGHTS. WIDTHS CAN BE JOINED WITH A JEANS-STYLE DOUBLE ROW OF ORANGE TOPSTITCHING.
- STRONG SEWING MACHINE NEEDLE (SOLD AS SUITABLE FOR DENIM)
- GREY THREAD, NORMAL THICKNESS
- NEEDLE FOR HANDSTITCHING
- PINS
- IRON
- TAPE MEASURE
- SCISSORS
- BIG, BRIGHT BUTTONS, ONE PER TAB
- SEWING MACHINE
- STAINLESS STEEL CURTAIN RAIL

PROJECT ONE

Denim tab-top curtains

Tab tops are really easy to make if you have a sewing machine. In fact, sewing is the best way to do it because denim is a heavyweight fabric, and very difficult to sew by hand. To jazz the denim up, sew a bright button at the bottom of each tab – you could also use metal stars, which are also very 'jeans'. The curtain rail is a stainless steel rail, which can be purchased from any DIY shop, although you could use copper piping instead. Line the curtains with a lightweight fabric that could be a plain colour, gingham or a floral print.

You can't go wrong with denim tab-top curtains, which are easy to make if you have a sewing machine.

HOW TO DO IT

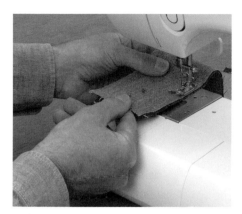

STEP 1 Cut a 160-mm-deep band the width of the fabric for the top of each curtain. Cut 2 260 mm x 80 mm strips per tab. They are spaced 100 mm apart, so calculate how many you will need for your window. Cut the curtain lengths to the drop, adding 20 mm for turnover and an 80-mm hem. Pin a 20-mm seam down the sides.

STEP 2 Stitch the side seams on the sewing machine using the grey thread. Turn over the hem and stitch this in the same way.

STEP 3 Place pairs of tabs together with right sides facing and stitch a seam on both sides. Turn them inside out and press flat with a hot iron. Fold them in half and press the fold.

STEP 4 Turn the curtains over and lay the tabs on top of the fabric with the raw ends slightly overlapping the top edge. Arrange them so that they are spaced 100mm apart. Check that the folded ends form a straight line and the tabs are exactly the same length. Make any length adjustments at the other end.

STEP 5 Lay the 160-mm deep band over the tabs on top of the curtain with the dark side facing upwards. Pin it in place keeping the tabs in their positions sandwiched between the two layers of fabric. Stitch all the way across, 20 mm inside the top edge. Turn the band over. The tabs are now at the top, fully enclosed in the contrasting band. Turn the edge over and top stitch the band to the curtain. Sew a bright button on each tab.

YOU WILL NEED:
- 1 PAIR OF OLD JEANS
- BIRO
- RULER
- SCISSORS
- PINS
- SEWING MACHINE WITH NEEDLE FOR DENIM
- STRONG THREAD IN ORANGE OR RED
- POLYESTER STUFFING

PROJECT TWO

Cushion cover from old jeans

This is one way to immortalise your favourite jeans or, if the idea of cutting them up is too painful to contemplate, you could buy a second-hand pair from a charity shop especially for the job. Extra trimmings can be added to spice the cushion up a bit – try a thick fringe, a broderie anglaise frill, velvet ribbons or some metal stars.

Denim refuses to go away and fashion designers have given up trying to ignore it, and now bring out new variations, decorations, colours, styles and hip labels. This cushion cover is made from old jeans.

HOW TO DO IT

STEP 1 Cut the legs of the jeans open along the front. Use a scalpel blade to cut the stitching of the back pockets. Lay the fabric out flat.

STEP 2 Cut out a square paper pattern and pin this to it. Cut out the two sides of the cushion in this way. Now re-stitch the pockets onto the centre of each of the denim squares using the strong orange or red thread.

STEP 4 Stuff the cushion with the polyester material and slipstitch the seam closed. Sew on any extra trimmings or pop the remote control into the pocket.

STEP 3 Lay the square down with right sides facing and pin a seam around the edge. Machine sew the seam with a double row of stitches leaving a 10-cm gap open for the stuffing. Snip the corners up to the stitching and turn the cushion cover the right way out. Press the cushion cover with a hot iron.

YOU WILL NEED:

- ONE VARNISHED
  WOODEN DINING
  CHAIR
- PAINT STRIPPER TO
  REMOVE THE OLD
  VARNISH
- SCRAPER
- RUBBER GLOVES
- SANDPAPER
- WIRE WOOL
- WHITE WATER-BASED
  PRIMER
- LIGHT PINK AND
  DARK PINK
  EMULSION PAINT
- 50-MM PAINTBRUSH
- 0.5 M FAKE FUR
  FABRIC
- STAPLE GUN
- FOAM PAD FOR SEAT
- CRAFT KNIFE
- CARPET-FITTING TAPE

PROJECT THREE

Pink pony chair

In this project, an old wooden chair is given a funky fur make-over. Old wooden dining room chairs don't cost very much, and you can have a lot of fun searching boot sales for the perfect specimen. Look for a nice-shaped back and a seat that's in good condition.

Give an old dining chair a denim and fake-fur make-over for the ultimate in groovy chic. You could choose denim fabric instead of the fake fur, and paint the chair a denim blue colour instead of pink.

HOW TO DO IT

STEP 1 Begin by sanding the chair smooth. Use paint stripper to remove any old paint.

STEP 2 Prime the woodwork of the chair with white acrylic primer.

STEP 3 Apply the first coat of the darker pink paint.

STEP 4 Lightly brush the second paler pink colour over the top of the first coat.

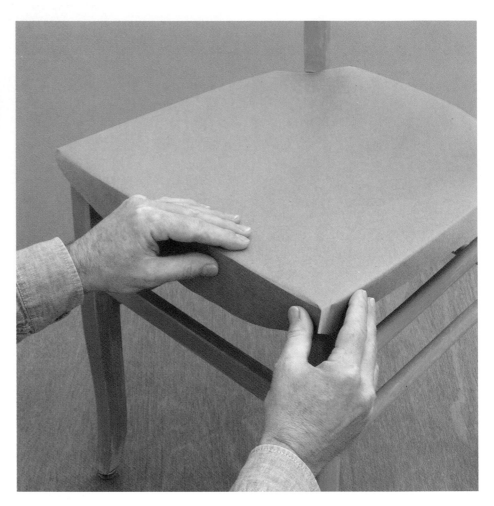

STEP 5 Gently wipe the paler top coat with a sponge to reveal parts of the dark pink paint.

STEP 6 When the paint is dry, fold brown paper over the seat, creasing at the edges, to make a template.

STEP 7 Cut out the paper template along the creases and place it on the foam pad. Cut round the template with a craft knife.

STEP 8 Lay the paper template on the fur fabric and cut round it, allowing approximately 50 mm for the turnovers.

STEP 9 Cut notches in the fur fabric so that it fits around the curved foam seat pad.

STEP 10 Apply carpet-fitting tape to the foam pad. Peel off the backing.

STEP 11 Press the fur fabric onto the sticky surface, making sure there are no creases.

STEP 12 Stick down alternate notches as you go, easing the fabric around the curved edges.

STEP 13 Apply carpet-fitting to the seat of the chair, and stick the covered cushion down.

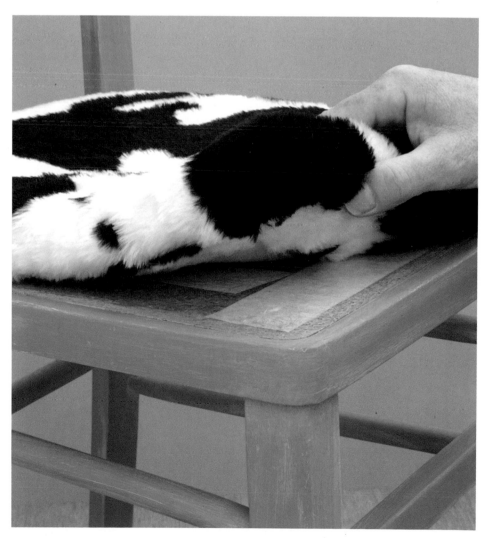

Children's bedrooms

Decorating a room for a child is brilliant fun. This is where you can experiment with paint effects, use bright colours and live out all your own childhood fantasies. Whether or not you have a free hand will depend upon the age of your child but you will know what they like best. All children have strong preferences for particular cartoon characters, animals, activities and colours from an early age. The best thing is that children love to feel special, and decorating a room especially for them is always a big success.

Think about the effect of colours before you choose the wall paint. Yellow is sunny and happy, while blue is relaxing and dreamy. Avoid red walls at all costs!

Children grow out of any cosily decorated nursery quicker than you might expect, but there's more than just redecoration to do to a children's room. Five things to consider when revamping a children's room are...

Decorating

If the room is being re-decorated for the first time since the nursery years then it is time for a big change. The most obvious and the cheapest way to change a room is by painting it a fresh new colour. Colour is known to affect us psychologically, and this may be worth investigating before you reach for the primary colours. If the room is also going to be a playroom and workroom then colour could be used to separate the areas. Green has calming, reassuring qualities, yellow is sunny, happy and warm, blue is relaxing and dreamy and for, obvious reasons, a good ceiling colour. Red is far too powerful a wall colour for a child's room but is good for fabrics and features. Boys often like orange, which is said to create a positive atmosphere, and all little girls have a pink phase, which may last for years: in fact some never grow out of it! Also try Roman blinds because they are easy to make, and the design is basic enough to withstand rough treatment. Make them in nice bright fabric backed with black-out lining material so that the room can be darkened for bedtime.

Play areas

A school-age child will need some sort of work area for model building and painting. Kids need to feel they can relax and make a mess, and that you will not make too much fuss if they spill and scatter things. For this reason it is a good idea to have mess-friendly flooring such as vinyl, lino, cork or laminated floorboards. Two colours of vinyl tiles can be laid as a chequerboard – white with yellow or grey looks good and not too overpowering. This sort of surface is good for all kinds of games as well – wheels speed across it and handstands can be done without slipping. Mats with a looped pile, more usually seen in the bathroom, are excellent because they come in lovely colours, are non-slip and can be cleaned in the washing machine. If your child is older and wants a more sophisticated style then go for cork or laminated floorboards with a soft rug by the bedside, and colourful rugs to laze on.

Lighting

Good lighting is equally important because children like to see what they are doing clearly. They will also make a lot more mess if they can't find what they're looking for! Lights need to be fixed on to surfaces, otherwise there is the risk that they will be knocked over and cause a fire. Fix angle-poise lights to the worktop or wall above it, simple wardrobe lights which come on when the door is opened and a wall light above the bed for reading. A central pendant light is a 'must' for brightening up the whole room, and small plug-in nightlights can be fitted into the wall sockets to give a soft glow.

Photographs

A frieze of pinboard on one wall will take care of all their favourite cartoon characters, pet pictures, party invitations, paintings and photographs. A wardrobe door or section of wall could be painted with blackboard paint to make an instant chalkboard. Make it big enough for a few friends to work on at the same time and supply loads of brightly coloured chalks. Also put a nice big mirror on the wall, and buy some easy-access frames so that photographs can be changed from time to time.

Books and toys

Keep bookshelves low down and accessible but also have high, out-of-reach cupboards for storage. This is especially useful when young children go through the stage of throwing everything out of drawers and cupboards. Buy a set of matching toy boxes on castors, which can be pushed away under the bed or into the bottom of a wardrobe. Also have separate places for paint brushes, construction kits, board games and dolls with their clothes and accessories. It may sound like hard work, but if everything has a place it is much easier to clear up. You can even try a row of pegs hung with orange plastic bags, which are great for small toys like bricks, cars and marbles. If you can make a game of putting things away it won't seem such a chore.

It is also worth buying or building a cupboard with deep shelves and a set of transparent plastic crates. Label each crate with the name of an article of clothing, using a picture and the word,

so that there is no confusion and everything stays in its own crate. Hooks on the back of the door or along the dado rail as shown in the project should take care of most things which you need to hang up. Child-sized wardrobes are also a good idea if you have a daughter with dresses – if the wardrobe is adult size then fit an extra rail lower down for her to reach and the top rail can be used for out-of-season clothes.

When we have children we often spend a great deal of time organising their activities, lessons and social events. It doesn't have to be this way all the time though, and they also need to relax. Large floor cushions, beanbag chairs or a small sofa-bed will also encourage them to think of the room as a place to snuggle down and think, read and listen to stories.

A bed with storage space underneath is a good way of saving floor space. If the storage will be on show, like this bedroom, a matching set of brightly coloured boxes will look fun, too.

THE PROJECTS
The projects on the following pages are a mixture of fun and function. Make sure you take your children's own preferences into account.

PROJECT ONE

Lining the walls with tongue-and-groove panelling

YOU WILL NEED:

- TONGUE-AND-GROOVE PANELLING TO FIT AROUND THE WALLS (MEASURE AND BUY PANELLING KIT PACKS TO FIT THE LENGTH REQUIRED)
- 3 LENGTHS OF 25-MM x 12-MM BATTENS FOR EACH WALL LENGTH
- SQUARE MOULDING TO FIT AROUND TOP OF PANELS (ONLY IF YOU ARE NOT FITTING THE PEG RAIL)
- 6-MM WALL PLUGS
- BOX OF No. 6 50-MM SCREWS
- BOX OF 25-MM PANEL PINS
- SMALL HAMMER
- DRILL WITH 6-MM BIT AND SPADE BIT FOR PEGS
- FINE NAIL PUNCH
- MITRE SAW, OR BLOCK WITH HANDSAW
- SCREWDRIVER
- LONG RULE WITH A SPIRIT LEVEL
- PENCIL

Wood panelling gives a very cosy, country feel to a room and the peg rail on the pages 136–137 is such a useful addition that you will wonder how you ever managed without it. If you buy the tongue-and-groove panelling in kit form it will be pre-cut and ready to fix to the wall. If you cut the lengths yourself you may like to make it slightly lower than usual, which has

the effect of scaling down the room to the child's size. If you are impatient for the boarded effect you can buy large panels of MDF which have been carved to give the effect of joined boards. They can simply be stuck to the wall using panel adhesive, although do bear in mind that removing them at a later date could affect the condition of the wall surface.

Tongue-and-groove panelling gives a children's room a cosy feel. The panelling can be bought in kit form and painted in your choice of colours. The hockey-stick moulding on the top makes a useful shelf, or for a wider shelf and row of pegs, see pages 136–137.

HOW TO DO IT

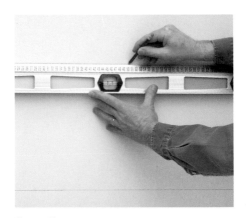

STEP 1 Using the rule with the spirit level, mark three positions for the battening on the wall to align with the top, middle and bottom of the panels.

STEP 2 Drill and insert wall plugs every 50 cm and then screw the battens onto the wall.

STEP 3 Beginning in one corner, place the end plank against the wall and check the vertical with the spirit level. Hammer a pin through the inside edge of the tongue, angled slightly inwards. Do this into all three battens. Use the nail punch with the hammer to drive the pinhead below the surface.

STEP 4 Fit the groove of the each subsequent plank into the tongue of the first. To ensure a tight fit place a spare piece of wood along the edge, and tap it with the hammer to prevent damage to the plank's tongue. Continue in the same way to complete the panelling.

STEP 5 Fit a narrow batten along the top edge of the panelling using panel pins and a nail punch.

STEP 6 Replace the skirting board, and then prime and paint the panelling in the colour of your choice. If you are also fitting the rail and shelf, continue as explained in the steps overleaf, fitting the rail along the top of the panelling. If not you will need to finish off the top of the panels with a square moulding. This can be screwed into the wall or stuck with panel adhesive.

YOU WILL NEED:

- 75-MM X 25-MM PAR SOFTWOOD TO FIT AROUND THE ROOM (MEASURE THE LENGTH REQUIRED)
- SHELF (THE SAME AMOUNT OF PAR SOFTWOOD AGAIN)
- SUPPORT BRACKETS FOR SHELF TO MATCH 75 MM DEPTH OF SHELF
- PEGS (EITHER BUY TURNED PEGS OR MAKE THEM FROM A LENGTH OF DOWEL. DECIDE HOW MANY YOU NEED FOR NOW, MORE CAN ALWAYS BE ADDED LATER)
- LONG RULE WITH SPIRIT LEVEL
- PENCIL
- DRILL
- 4-MM BIT FOR CLEARANCE HOLES
- 6-MM BIT FOR WALL
- SPADE BIT FOR PEGS
- 6-MM WALL PLUGS SUITABLE FOR YOUR KIND OF WALL
- PENCIL

PROJECT TWO

Fitting a peg rail and shelf

This can either be a continuation of the tongue-and-groove panelling project on the previous pages (pages 134–135), or a project on its own. If you decide against the panelling, you may not want to fit the peg rail and shelf on more than one wall. The instructions allow for this, and explain the order and technique rather than giving exact measurements.

A row of pegs can make clearing up fun. Hang a row of brightly coloured bags on the pegs to put small toys like bricks, cars or marbles, or hang the toys directly on the pegs themselves. The shelf above offers even more storage space.

HOW TO DO IT

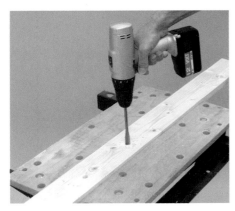

STEP 1 Cut the peg rail plank to fit the wall lengths, mitring the ends for a neat fit in the corners and at any joins. Check and mark the rail position on the wall with a spirit level. Drill clearance holes in the planks then mark, drill and plug the wall, and screw the peg rail in place.

STEP 2 Use the spade bit to drill holes for the pegs and then apply wood glue to their ends before pushing them firmly into the rail. If the pegs are to be painted different colours, it may be easier to do this before you fit them.

STEP 3 If you are adding a shelf to the top of the peg rail, do so now. Screw the peg rail to the wall.

STEP 4 Screw the shelf to the peg rail and through into the wall batten. Prime and paint.

YOU WILL NEED:
- WHITE WOOD PRIMER
- 2 BRIGHT-COLOURED MATCH POTS OF EMULSION PLUS CLEAR VARNISH, OR 2 SATINWOOD OR EGGSHELL COLOURS
- WATER-BASED BLACKBOARD PAINT
- SMALL FOAM ROLLER AND TRAY
- PAINT BRUSHES
- SANDPAPER

PROJECT THREE

Painting MDF furniture and using blackboard paint

An ideal project to encourage your children's writing skills (or at least their noughts and crosses!) This is a small painting project that will make a big difference. Incorporate your children's two favourite colours to make it personal. You could apply the idea to any piece of furniture you already own, find a second-hand piece to make-over, or buy an unpainted MDF blank. Blanks are nicely designed pieces of furniture made especially for people who enjoy applying the paint themselves. They are sold by mail order, and the money saved by not painting them is reflected in the price. You will find an address in the directory at the back of the book.

HOW TO DO IT

STEP 1 Sand the old paint to create a good surface for the paint to key into.

STEP 2 Prime the whole unit using a white water-based paint.

STEP 3 If the furniture has panels, paint as shown. If not, draw a square shape across the front and edge it with masking tape.

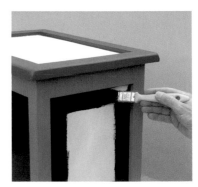

STEP 4 Apply two coats of blackboard paint and wait until dry before removing the tape.

YOU WILL NEED:
- 50-CM x 50-CM CUSHION (COVER AND INNER CUSHION PAD)
- 40 CM x 40 CM WHITE COTTON FABRIC (A COTTON PILLOW CASE)
- THREAD TO STITCH PRINT ONTO THE CUSHION COVER

PROJECT FOUR

Making photocopied fun cushions

T-shirt printing is available at most photocopying shops, and any image not protected by copyright laws can be photocopied onto a special film and transferred onto fabric. The image could be a photograph of your dog, a holiday snap, or an original drawing, cut-out or pattern. Take a plain white square of cotton fabric to the photocopying shop and ask them to transfer the image on to the fabric, then take it home and make up a cushion. The transfer film can also be bought for home use with a computer scanner and printer.

HOW TO DO IT

STEP 1 Cut out a square of white cotton fabric measuring roughly 40 cm x 40 cm. Choose an image to be photo-copied and trim it to a square shape.

STEP 2 Mark the size and position for the print on the white cotton fabric, and take this to the photocopiers. Ask them to enlarge and print the image onto your fabric.

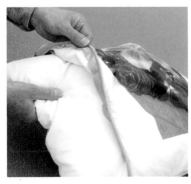

STEP 3 Fold back a small hem on the printed fabric and pin it to the front of the cushion cover. Slipstitch by hand or machine stitch.

Fantasy bedroom

Parents often find that having a young child gives them the opportunity to rediscover their artistic side which may have been neglected since they left school. It's fantastic when you realise that the time has come to put all those skills learned in woodwork, art and design lessons to good use.

A lot of the most exciting decorating programmes on TV create rooms which are a mixture of window dressing and stage design adapted for the home. Children's bedrooms can be treated in the same way, and all you need are basic skills, time and imagination. There is no reason why their beds have to look like beds – so long as they are safe and comfortable to sleep in, they can be anything from caves to castles. The same approach can be used to transform the whole room into a complete fantasy world.

Children's bedrooms are often also their playrooms, so fun is a number one priority. But apart from safety and comfort, there are no rules when it comes to decorating children's rooms, so let your imagination run wild!

MDF beds

Children's beds can be expensive, but why buy one when you can make a very special one from MDF? The design chosen for the project on the following pages is a castle, and whether you have a little sleeping beauty or knight in shining armour the bed is sure to be a hit.

The one very good reason why MDF is so popular is that it has no grain. When you work with natural wood the direction of the grain is extremely important, particularly when cutting and planing. The main reason for this is that wood splits along the grain and if, for instance, you insert a row of screws in a line along the grain the wood is very likely to split. Softwood is most prone to splitting because it is harvested from fast-growing trees so the grain is less dense than with hardwood, which comes from slow-growing trees.

MDF is short for medium density fibreboard. It is made from small, even-sized particles of wood which have been mixed with a chemical compound to bind them together before being compacted into sheets. You should always wear a mask when sawing through MDF because the dust contains those binding chemical compounds, which can be harmful, and it is best not to do the cutting work in your child's bedroom where the fine dust will be difficult to clear away completely. Once MDF is cut out and painted it presents no greater health risk than any other construction material. The good news is that MDF can be cut into all kinds of shapes with a jigsaw. A bed like a castle is easy!

The castle theme

Once you have made the bed, turn your attention to other areas in the room to extend the castle theme. If you have shelving it can be edged with strips cut out in the shape of battlements, and the bedcover could be decorated with appliqué shields or knight's heraldic flags. Curtain poles can have arrow-head finials (securely screwed to the wall!), and the toy chest could be made to look like a king's treasure chest.

If you are making the castle for a princess, she will probably also like the idea of a climbing rose winding its way up the battlements, with a

THE PROJECTS

The projects on the following pages show how to make and paint a castle bed. Some battlement shelving, a heraldic bedcover and a king's treasure chest will complete the castle theme.

painted crown about her pillow and a silky bedcover to sleep under. Think of Queen Guinevere in Camelot, where ladies were wrapped in velvet trimmed with lace. If she is more of a Joan of Arc, it might be wiser to stick to battlements and suits of armour!

Role play is a favourite children's activity, so if their bedroom is designed like a stage, with a number of different scenes and settings, they'll be in heaven!

YOU WILL NEED:
- 2 SIDES 18-MM MDF, 2 M x 1 M
- 2 ENDS 18-MM MDF, 85 CM x 1 M
- 4 LEGS 50-MM x 50-MM PAR, 40 CM
- 2 SIDE BATTENS 38-MM x 38-MM PAR, 1.9 M
- 8 SLATS FOR BASE 25-MM x 15-CM PAR, 81 CM
- WOOD GLUE
- WOOD FILLER
- SANDPAPER
- BOX OF 50-MM No. 6 SCREWS
- FACE MASK
- JIGSAW
- DRILL WITH 2-MM, 4-MM AND COUNTERSINK BIT
- SCREWDRIVER
- TAPE MEASURE
- LONG RULER
- PENCIL
- COMBINATION SQUARE

MDF is a perfect material for cutting out a castle's battlements. You could choose a different kind of building if you're not so keen on the castle idea.

PROJECT ONE

The castle bed

The plan for the castle bed tells you what you need and exactly how it is made. This is the first stage of the project, and in the next stage there are ideas for how it can be painted. If you are keen to make a bed but not so keen on the castle idea then the plan could be adapted. You could use the same basic construction method but change the cut-out shape to give the bed a different theme. Cars and engines are always popular with boys. If your child has a favourite story or cartoon film then that would be a good place to look for inspiration.

HOW TO DO IT

This makes a bed that will fit a standard 80-mm-wide mattress.

STEP 1 Support the MDF between two trestles or tables and draw the cut-outs on the ends and the sides. Draw positional guidelines on the sides for the legs and the side battens. Use the long rule to draw them as continuous pencil lines.

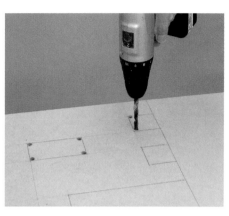

STEP 2 Drill holes in the corners of each of the cut-outs to access the saw blade.

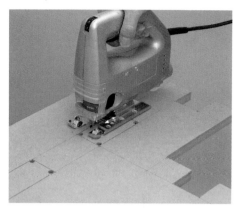

STEP 3 Wear a mask! Use the jigsaw carefully to cut out the shapes, then use sandpaper to round off the edges paying particular attention to the sides of the bed where the child will be climbing in and out.

STEP 4 Drill the pilot holes and countersink holes for the screws.

STEP 5 Glue and screw the legs and side battens in place.

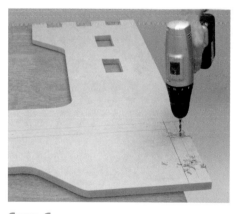

STEP 6 Draw positional guides on the two ends for the legs, and to mark where the bed ends meet the sides on the MDF. Drill pilot holes and countersink the screws.

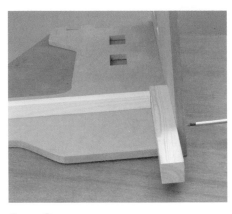

STEP 7 Drill, glue and screw the MDF panels to the legs of the bed.

STEP 8 Glue and screw the ends to the sides.

STEP 9 Space out the base slats (mattress supports) and then drill pilot holes, and glue and screw them to the bed. Fill all the countersink holes and sandpaper smooth once the filler has set.

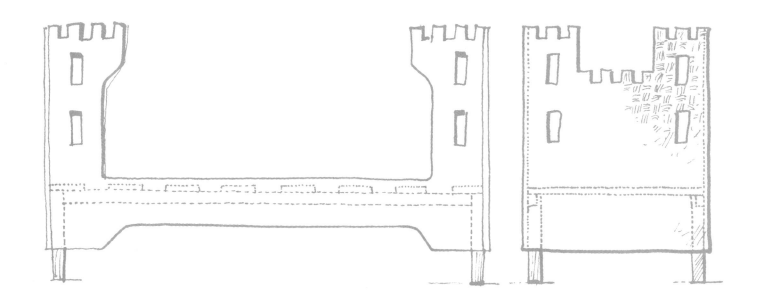

Follow these guidelines when you are making up your castle bed. Remember to measure everything properly and use a spirit level to check that everything is flush.

YOU WILL NEED:

- **FOAM OFFCUTS ROUGHLY 50 MM SQUARE**
- **PLATE**
- **SMALL FOAM ROLLER AND TRAY**
- **EMULSION PAINT IN DARK AND LIGHT GREY**
- **CLEAR MATT VARNISH**

PROJECT TWO
Painting the castle bed

The method described here is just one way to paint the castle bed. You may prefer to paint it freehand, or all in one colour (see page 142). This method shows a quick and easy way of giving the castle bed the appearance of weathered brickwork. You could use this method with another pale colour, such as light blue.

HOW TO DO IT

STEP 1 Cut three or four foam squares into rough stone shapes. They can vary in size and be rounded off at the corners.

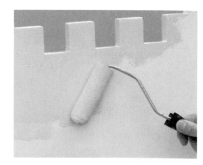

STEP 2 Use the foam roller to paint the whole bed in a base coat of light grey.

STEP 3 Thin the darker emulsion with water, 2 parts paint to 1 part water, then use the foam blocks to build up the castle brickwork. Cover with a coat of clear varnish when dry.

Nursery

When it comes to preparing for a new arrival our instincts are like any animal's. We want to make a cosy nest and have everything ready for the big day. Nature is a wonderful thing, and even if you have never looked twice at a frieze of fluffy bunnies or frolicking lambs before, you will find the choice is suddenly actually a major one! A baby opens up a whole new world and it's amazing that something so small needs that much stuff. In truth they don't but we do, and as long as we keep spending, manufacturers will keep coming up with new ideas to make life with a baby easier and more pleasant.

These flimsy curtains may look nice, but they will make it impossible to encourage a baby to sleep in the daylight.

Decorating a nursery for a first baby is one of life's luxuries. The baby won't mind how you decorate it, but it gives expectant parents something positive to do, and there are lots of things to look out for.

Colours

If you already know the sex of your baby, you may want to follow a traditional pink or blue colour scheme, or the usual alternative, which has always been pale yellow. One good reason for sticking to these colours is that they are the colours of most products, presents and accessories for babies. Strong primary colours like red, yellow and blue are great for later on but they seem very harsh for a nursery. There are more gentle contemporary colours if you wish to avoid the pinks and blues such as moss green, pale sea green, lavender, apricot and buttery cream.

It may be difficult to imagine, but your baby will soon be a rampaging toddler and it is worth keeping this in mind when you decorate. Try to choose colours and styles that will either be appropriate later on, or which can be added to or adapted for a growing child.

Windows

The most important thing you need to know about nursery windows is that they need to have curtains or blinds that block out the light completely. This can be done by lining curtains with black or navy fabric or using special black-out lining fabric. Flimsy muslin curtains will do nothing to convince a baby that it's time to sleep if the sun is still shining outside!

Roller blinds are fine for babies before they begin
to investigate the way things work, but can be
something of a hazard later on when the pulls are
grabbed too hard or suddenly let go of so that
they shoot out of reach. Roman blinds fold up
and down and are a better bet because they don't
need stiffening, can be lined with black-out and
are surprisingly easy to make.

Changing

Babies generate an incredible amount of washing
and you will need one or two laundry bins. Two
will enable you to sort out the more urgent
towelling hot wash from the rest when you
change your baby. Changing nappies and baby
clothes can be a backbreaking task if you are
constantly leaning over, and it will be a lot easier
if you have a changing table with everything you
need close at hand. Baby clothes can be kept
handy in drawers or baskets below with cotton
wool, wipes and nappies all being within easy
reach on the table top.

Sitting

In the early months it is a good idea to have a
comfortable chair to sit in while you're feeding
the baby. Have a small table with a lamp to read
by as well because you may want to consult any
baby books you may have or just need
somewhere safe to put a drink down. Once your
baby begins to crawl and climb up, everything
that could topple over like a small table with a
lamp should be removed from the room to
prevent accidents.

Lighting

Central lights are the best and safest option in
the nursery. Look out for a fabulous lampshade
that will give your baby something to gaze at.
Safe nightlights made specially for a child's room

can also be great fun, especially the ones that
turn round and project images on the walls –
babies love them.

Sleeping

Deciding whether to buy a crib or a cot is a
personal one. A cot is more practical because it
will last for about three years, though tiny babies
do look lost in them, but a crib is so sweet and it
is almost impossible to wear one out. Full-sized
cots are adjustable to three different heights. If
you decide to use one from the start, have it at
the highest level to avoid too much bending and
move it down as soon as your baby starts pulling
up on the bars.

**Pinks and blues
are the colours of
most baby products,
presents and
accessories, so
it makes sense to
use these colours
for the walls.**

PROJECT ONE

Painting a gingham wall

Gingham is one of the freshest fabrics around and it will never, ever go out of fashion. This project shows how to customise a small foam roller and give the nursery walls a gingham effect. You can do this on a coloured background if you prefer, but white is traditional and always makes a room look bigger and brighter. Most nursery borders look good with gingham, and if you buy one first you can co-ordinate the colours.

Gingham made easy – a simple trick with a small foam roller can transform a nursery wall, making it look bigger and brighter.

HOW TO DO IT

STEP 1 Wrap the masking tape around the middle of the roller, dividing it into three equal parts.

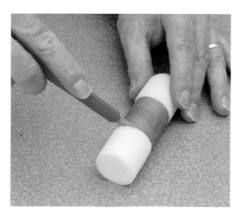

STEP 2 Cut down to the middle of the roller in a straight line following the edge of the tape. Turn the roller and cut all the way around, then once across between the lines.

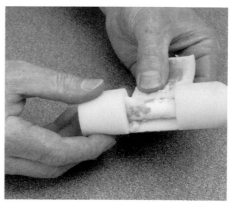

STEP 3 Peel off the middle foam section then peel off the masking tape.

STEP 4 Mix the wallpaper paste following the instructions on the pack, and then mix it half and half with the emulsion paint in the roller tray.

STEP 5 Hang the plumb line from the top of the wall to give you a vertical guide to follow. Run the roller through the paint/wallpaper paste mixture and begin painting in one corner, applying a medium pressure and continuing to within about 5 cm of the skirting board. This final bit can be applied filled in with the offcut from the roller. Continue in this way to complete all the vertical stripes

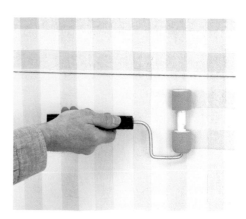

STEP 6 Place the spirit level on the wall and make some small guide marks for the first horizontal band of striping. The next stripes can be aligned with the first, but check with the level on each alternate row so that you don't drift away from the horizontal.

YOU WILL NEED:
• 1 BASE CUT FROM
18-MM MDF – THIS
SHOULD BE 78 CM
DEEP (FROM FRONT
TO BACK) AND THE
WIDTH OF THE CHEST
OF DRAWERS PLUS
5 MM ON EACH SIDE
• 1 BATTEN 50-MM X
25-MM, THE WIDTH
OF THE MDF
• 2 SIDES 15 -M X
25-MM X 78-CM PAR
SOFTWOOD
• 1 BACK 15-CM X
25-MM PAR
SOFTWOOD, WIDTH
OF CHEST OF
DRAWERS PLUS 10 MM
• JIGSAW
• PANEL PINS
• WOOD GLUE
• NAIL PUNCH
• FILLER
• DRILL WITH 2-MM
PILOT BIT AND
COUNTERSINK BIT
• 50-MM No. 6 SCREWS
• SANDPAPER
• PAINT

PROJECT TWO

Making a removable changing table top

The first few months with a new baby can be very tiring, and it is impossible to imagine how backbreaking nappy changing can be if you are constantly bending over. This project shows you can make a table top which can sit on a chest of drawers, a small desk or even a single kitchen unit at the right height, to make nappy changing a thousand times easier. It has been designed to be used lengthways with the back pushed up against the wall, and the supporting chest of drawers or desk pulled forward so that the front is level with the edge of the unit. Any foam-padded, sponge-cleanable changing mat will fit into the wooden frame. The exact dimensions will depend upon the size of the piece of furniture you are using as a base.

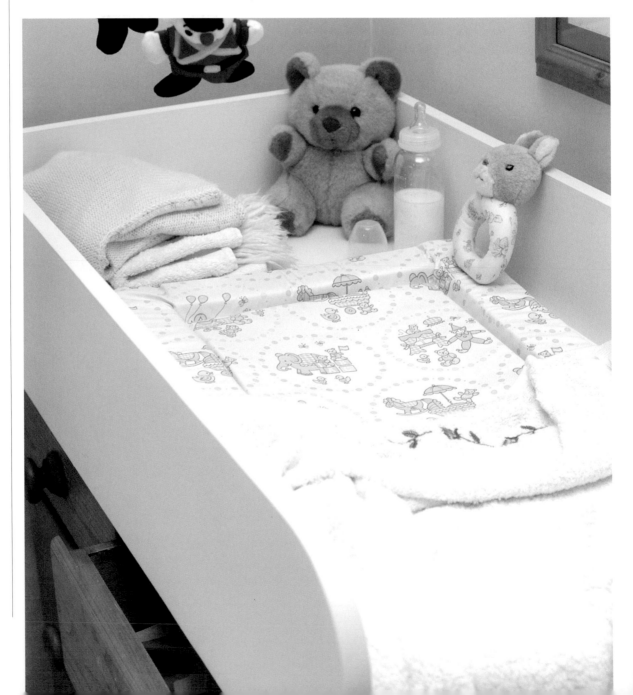

A portable table top
for nappy changing
makes the task far
less backbreaking.
Decide which piece of
furniture you will use
underneath before
working out the
dimensions.

HOW TO DO IT

STEP 1 Mark the base position on the back board and mark, screw, drill and countersink the screws.

STEP 2 Place the top on your base in line with the front, and draw a line to mark the back edge.

STEP 3 Draw location guides on the base for the sides and the back. Drill pilot and countersunk holes for the screws.

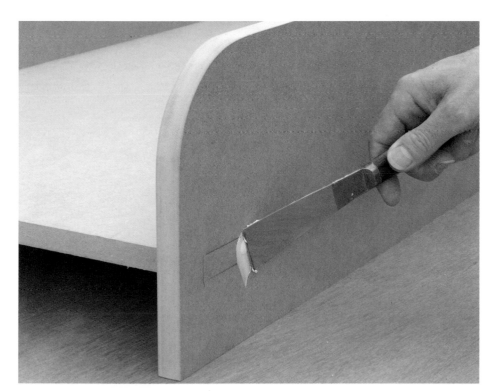

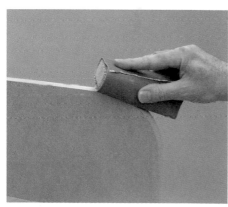

STEP 5 Sandpaper all the edges to round them off, and then prime and paint the unit.

STEP 4 Cut the rounded corners on the front of both sides with a jigsaw. Glue and screw the back to the base from below, followed by both sides. Fill the screw holes with filler.

YOU WILL NEED:
- **FISHING LINE**
- **1 30-CM LENGTH OF STRAIGHT WIRE**
- **2 20-CM LENGTHS OF STRAIGHT WIRE**
- **SCRAP OF STIFF CARD**
- **SCISSORS**
- **BIRO**
- **COLOURED FELT**
- **COTTON WOOL**
- **NEEDLE AND THREAD**
- **GLUE**
- **SEQUINS AND SMALL BLACK BUTTONS FOR EYES**
- **HOOK FOR HANGING**

PROJECT THREE

Fish mobile

There is one other essential ingredient to keep a baby happy in the nursery, and that is a mobile. It is made from simple felt shapes hung from three mobile wires on nylon thread. Make sure that the mobile is always well out of the baby's reach.

This colourful fish mobile, made out of simple felt shapes, should provide a welcome distraction for a baby in his or her cot.

HOW TO DO IT

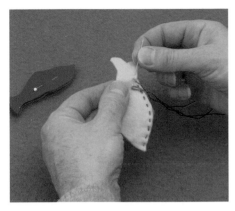

STEP 1 Draw a fish shape onto a piece of card and cut it out. Use this as a template to draw 10 fish shapes on the felt.

STEP 2 Cut out the fish and put them together in pairs. Sew around the outside leaving a small gap for the stuffing. Stuff each fish with a small amount of cotton wool, and slipstitch the gap closed. Glue the sequins onto the middle of the fish as scales. Sew two small buttons on each one for eyes.

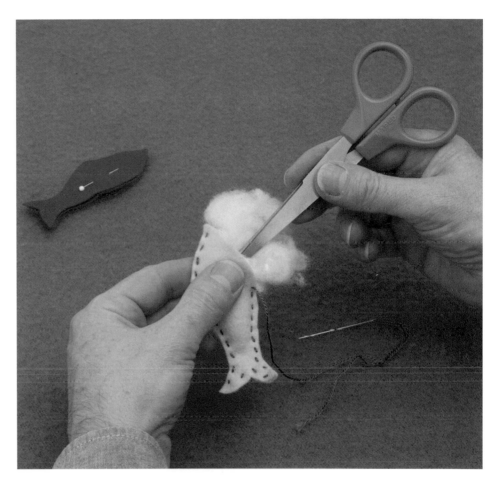

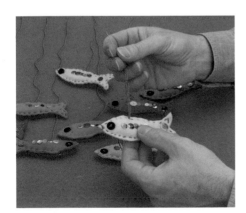

STEP 3 Cut one length of fishing line to hang the mobile at the correct height. Then cut 4 x 30-cm lengths, 2 x 20-cm lengths and 2 x 15-cm lengths.

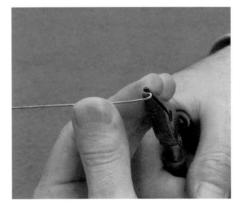

STEP 4 Twist the wires over at both ends making loops. Thread the fishing line onto a needle and attach a line to each fish (as shown). Tie the lines onto the wires (as shown). Screw a hook to the ceiling and hang the fishy mobile over the cot or changing area.

Bathrooms

Today's bathrooms are more than simply a place to wash. They have become sanctuaries for pampering and indulgence, a tranquil retreat in which to relax and unwind, a beauty salon in your own home. As one of the first rooms you see in the morning and one of the last you see at night, it's no wonder its decor and style can make such a difference to how you start or end the day. This section shows how to transform your bathroom into one of two different styles, Traditional or Contemporary, before looking specifically at the shower room. Choose a style, choose a project, and go full steam ahead!

Traditional bathroom

The bathrooms which we now tend to think of as being traditional are actually early 20th century in style, when the bathroom first became a feature in ordinary people's houses. Modern Europeans were a bit slow on the uptake as far as bathrooms went, but the Romans long before had stunning baths and flushing toilets. There was a gap until the first bath was installed in the White House in 1851, and there was no bathroom in Buckingham Palace when Queen Victoria began her reign in 1837. By the end of it though, all kinds of bathroom fixtures had been invented, including stand-up showers, short and long baths, flushing toilets, mixer taps and heated towel rails. And now there has never been more choice in bathroom fittings and fixtures, so whatever your idea of traditional may be, you can satisfy every whim.

A freestanding bathtub positioned in the centre of the room with an old-style shower above looks wonderful. If you're buying an old iron bath, check your floor joists are strong enough to support it.

With such a huge choice of bathroom fittings and fixtures, it's a good idea to make a list of the things you would like in your traditional bathroom before you begin redecorating. Nine things to consider are...

Planning

If you are planning a complete bathroom refit then this is a good opportunity to move things around. Just because the bath is against one wall doesn't mean that that is the only place for it. The bathroom may have been planned by someone with no imagination or design skills, and now is your big chance to give it a complete new look. The best way to begin is to visit a bathroom showroom – the most upmarket one you can find – and pick up all the latest brochures. Always start by looking at the best designs and work backwards to something which suits your budget. That way you will immediately be able to spot the best features in the cheaper range, and see where savings can be made without any loss of style.

Some bathroom brochures include a planning section, but if not you can make one yourself using graph paper and scaled down cut-outs of the main fixtures. Mark the position of the window and door on your plan, and then see if the bath, basin or toilet are in the best places. If the door takes up space when open, perhaps it could be re-hung to open outwards or even be moved further along the wall. Pipes and the electricity supply can always be re-routed if a new arrangement makes more sense. And if you have a large bathroom, the bath could be moved away from the wall into the middle of the room. Plan the lighting at the beginning of the project, and make the most of any natural light by painting the window frames white and fitting blinds into the frame recess. If you have a window with a view that is not overlooked, position the bath so that you can enjoy the view when you're in it. Mirrors should be placed in both useful and flattering positions!

Old v New Fixtures and Fittings

If you choose a period-style bathroom suite you can opt for the real thing or a reproduction version. Many companies make reconditioned baths and basins, or you could visit an architectural salvage yard, which is great fun and usually has lower prices than antique shops. Before buying an old iron bath you must find out whether your bathroom floor joists are strong enough to support

Original wooden floorboards look lovely in a traditional bathroom, either stripped and painted with a waterproof floor paint, or simply stripped and varnished.

its weight plus 110 kg of water plus a person! Old taps may look wonderful but might not have the right size pipe connectors for modern plumbing, so do find out what it will cost to have them updated before celebrating your bargain buy. Since most old styles of fixtures and fittings have been copied it is often best to buy the new versions and attach them to the bath. Old lace shelf-edgings, glass bottles, mirror frames and shelves add to the atmosphere without costing a fortune. And treat yourself, at least once, to expensive bottled bath products to display on the shelves – you can always refill them with the supermarket version later on!

Showers

A separate shower room is ideal and it does not have to be much bigger than the average cubicle, but for most people a shower has to be fitted into the bathroom, either as a self-contained unit or over the bath. There are lots of options, and it is best to get advice from an expert. Begin by asking a plumber which system is best suited to your home. It will depend upon several factors

including the siting of your cold water tank, the water pressure and your boiler type. Armed with this information you will be able to pass on the technical details to the sales staff, and confine your efforts to your favourite style. If you are fitting a power shower unit over a bath then a shower curtain will not be enough to protect the surroundings, and you will need to have a panel or folding screen, which can be quite pricey.

Electricity

Never be tempted to do a DIY electrical job in the bathroom. Wait until you've got a few jobs that need doing and then employ a qualified electrician to install new fittings and check old ones at the same time. By law all switches have to be outside the bathroom, and an electrician will make sure that all the correct procedures are followed.

Lighting

Bathroom light fittings must have suitable sealed units for safety reasons. All switches must be pull-cords, and all fittings must be kept well clear of any potential splashes. The lighting should create a relaxing atmosphere with efficient illumination where it is most needed.

Walls

Steamy bathrooms need walls with water-resistant surfaces, which is why glazed tiles are so practical around basins, toilets and baths. The damp that often occurs in bathrooms happens when they are not very well ventilated in winter and condensation becomes a problem. You can buy special paints for bathrooms made with added fungicides to combat mould, but if you don't want to introduce such chemicals into the atmosphere then stick to an oil-based eggshell or gloss paint, or an emulsion sealed with waterproof varnish.

One of the projects in this section shows how to line a bathroom with tongue and groove panelling. Although it is an old idea it has now become the most popular alternative to tiling. It is not necessary to remove old tiles when you change to panelling, or indeed when you change tiles as the new ones can simply be laid over the existing ones. If you are re-tiling, do it in a brickwork pattern to give the tiles a brand new look. If you want to refresh the tiling on a tight budget, use tile paint to change the colour or simply re-grout the existing tiles to give them a fresh new look.

Floors

Bathroom floors get wetter than any other floor in the home, especially if you have young children, and there is no doubt that non-slip, sheet vinyl is the best option. This can be sealed along the edges with silicone so that no water can seep underneath. The range of patterns and prices is huge, and there will be something to suit all tastes and budgets. Small bathrooms could be tackled with off-cuts, so get measuring before you visit a showroom and ask if they have a selection of roll ends. Your choice will certainly be limited to what is available, but do have a look. If you prefer carpets, choose one with a rot-proof latex backing and use a bathmat with waterproof backing as well. Floating wooden floors are not suitable for bathrooms, but original wooden floorboards look lovely stripped and varnished or painted with a waterproof floor paint. A stencilled pattern or different shades or colours for the border create further interest.

Wood panelling is an old idea, but for those not keen on tiling it is the most popular choice. The panelling can be laid over existing tiles to save work in removing them.

Storage

All your hard work will be wasted if the bathroom shelves and bath surround become cluttered with shampoo bottles, shavers and toothbrushes. Assess your space and make the most of any dead areas for storage. They include wall-to-ceiling space above the toilet, above the end of the bath, and the wall under the sink. If extra towels are to be kept in the bathroom they can be folded and put on display.

Essential luxury

A bathroom is a room for self-indulgence, somewhere to relax and recharge your batteries. It is a room to indulge in small luxuries and they should be included in the budget. Scented candles, bubble bath, a large fluffy towel on a heated rail and the right bath mat can make you feel as pampered as any supermodel. Remember that everything in the bathroom does not have to have hard edges and, if you can, find room for an upholstered chair to help create a relaxed atmosphere.

THE PROJECTS

The four projects on the following pages will help achieve a traditional background in your bathroom. Some period-style fixtures and fittings and a big pile of fluffy towels should do the rest.

Cupboards can help hIde cleaning materials, spare toilet rolls and toiletry clutter in your bathroom. Look for some dead space in the bathroom where you could fit a small freestanding or wall-mounted unit.

YOU WILL NEED:

MATERIALS

• TONGUE AND GROOVE
  PANELLING TO FIT
  AROUND THE WALLS.
  (MEASURE AND BUY
  PANELLING KITS TO FIT
  THE LENGTH
  REQUIRED)
• THREE LENGTHS OF
  25-MM X 12-MM
  BATTENS FOR EACH
  WALL LENGTH
• SHELF 75-MM X 25-
  MM PAR SOFTWOOD
  TO FIT AROUND THE
  ROOM (MEASURE THE
  LENGTH REQUIRED)
• SUPPORT BRACKETS
  FOR THE SHELF TO BE
  SPACED 60 CM APART
• 6-MM WALL PLUGS
• BOX OF No. 6, 50-MM
  SCREWS
• BOX OF 25-MM PANEL
  PINS
• SMALL HAMMER
• DRILL WITH 6-MM
  AND 2-MM PILOT BIT
• FINE NAIL PUNCH
• MITRE SAW OR BLOCK
  WITH HANDSAW
• SCREWDRIVER
• LONG RULE WITH A
  SPIRIT LEVEL
• PENCIL

PROJECT ONE

Lining the walls with tongue-and-groove panelling

This is a lovely style for a bathroom which can be given a country or seaside accent, depending upon the colour and paint finish used. You may even like the idea of staining the wood dark brown to give it a distinctly masculine style. The shelf around the top of the panelling can have hooks screwed into it for hanging up small hand towels and flannels.

Wooden panelling can be customised to the style you want by the choice of paint colour – blues and greens for a seaside theme, or earthy browns and creams for a country feel. Dark-brown wood stain will give it a masculine style.

HOW TO DO IT

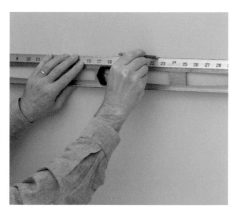

STEP 1 Use the rule with the spirit level to mark three positions for the battening on the wall to align with the top, middle and bottom of the panels. Drill and insert wall plugs spaced 50 cm apart, and then screw the battens onto the wall.

STEP 2 Beginning in one corner, place the end plank against the wall and check the vertical with the spirit level. Hammer a pin through the inside edge of the tongue angled slightly inwards. Do this into all three battens. Use the nail punch with the hammer to drive the pinhead below the surface.

STEP 3 Fit the groove of the next plank into the tongue of the first. To ensure a tight fit, place a spare piece of wood along the edge and tap it with the hammer. Continue in the same way to complete the panelling. Planks will almost certainly need to be cut down to fit at the corners. Draw a line where this is required, clamp the plank in the jaws of a workbench and cut with a handsaw or powersaw.

STEP 4 Use a nail punch to knock the pinheads into the timber.

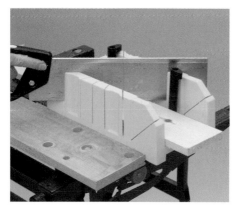

STEP 5 Cut the shelf planks to fit the wall lengths, mitring the ends for a neat fit in the corners and at any joins. Check and mark the shelf position on the wall with a spirit level. Drill pilot holes in the planks and the panels for the brackets.

STEP 6 Screw the brackets into the front of the panelling and down through the shelf into the top of the brackets. Prime and paint with gloss, or emulsion sealed with marine-quality varnish.

YOU WILL NEED:

- STRIP OF HARDBOARD ABOUT 7.5 CM DEEP. MEASURE AROUND THE BASIN FOR THE LENGTH
- 2 x 12-CM BATTENS 50 MM x 25 MM
- 4 NO. 10, 75-MM SCREWS
- 7-MM WALL PLUGS
- HARDBOARD PINS
- CURTAIN FABRIC – FOR GATHERED EFFECT BUY DOUBLE THE WIDTH
- STRONG SELF-ADHESIVE VELCRO
- STRONG CLEAR GLUE TO ATTACH TRIMMING
- DRILL WITH 7-MM MASONRY BIT
- SMALL HAMMER
- STAPLE GUN (ONLY IF YOU'RE NOT USING VELCRO)

PROJECT TWO

Hanging a curtain below a basin

This project makes a pretty addition to a traditional bathroom, and also provides a concealed storage area below the basin for cleaning materials. Basins are made to many different designs, some rounded and others square at the front. Hardboard is used here to make a curved strip which fixes on to the wall behind the basin. The curtain is attached with strong Velcro, but for a quick fix you could use staples instead, and then cover the staples with a braid or ribbon held in place with strong glue. This will make it harder to remove and wash.

A simple curved strip of hardboard provides a curtain rail around a basin, creating extra storage space beneath the basin as well as an attractive bathroom feature.

HOW TO DO IT

STEP 1 Mark the positions for the two wall battens just below the outside edge of the basin using a ruler and pencil.

STEP 2 Drill two holes to secure each batten and fit them with wall plugs. Screw the battens in position

STEP 4 Attach the sticky side of the velcro to the hardboard, and the other side to the curtains. Allow one to overlap the other by about 3 cm in the front so that the curtains don't gape (or staple the fabric to the hardboard, and then glue on a braid or ribbon to cover the staples).

STEP 3 Dampen the hardboard to make it more flexible and then attach it shiny side out, below the sink. Attach one side of the hardboard to the batten with the pins, then bend the hardboard into a curve and attach the other side to the other batten in the same way.

YOU WILL NEED:
• SUGAR SOAP AND
  CLOTH TO CLEAN
  THE BOARDS
• AN ELECTRIC SANDER
  WITH COARSE GRADE
  PAPER
• NAIL PUNCH
  AND HAMMER
• PRIMER
• THREE SHADES OF
  BLUE WOODWASH
  OR EMULSION PAINT
• PAINT BRUSHES
• MARINE STRENGTH
  CLEAR VARNISH
• SMALL ROLLER
  AND TRAY

PROJECT THREE

Painting floorboards

If you live in an old house you will most likely have floorboards in the bathroom. A painted wooden floor looks nice but a striped wooden floor is even better. The idea is to take one main colour and two shades of it, one slightly deeper and one slightly lighter, giving an effect of subtle shading. Start painting at the far wall and work back towards the door.

Original wooden floorboards look great painted in stripes contrasting three shades of the same colour.

HOW TO DO IT

STEP 1 Sweep the floor and then check all the nails, firmly tapping down any that protrude using the nail punch and a hammer.

STEP 2 Use the electric sander to get rid of any rough areas that could cause splinters. Don't spend too much time doing this because the paint and varnish will add a smooth finish.

STEP 3 Scrub the floor with a sugar soap solution and leave it to dry.

STEP 4 Begin painting with the darker shade next to the far skirting board. Paint the next board in the main colour (this is likely to be used elsewhere in the room).

STEP 5 Paint the third colour and then repeat this sequence back across the room towards the door. It will be easier to paint the last three boards once the rest have dried, letting you reach into the corners and up to the skirting board.

STEP 6 Finally apply at least two coats of clear varnish, allowing the correct drying time between coats.

YOU WILL NEED:
- WINDOW CLEANER
- PAPER TOWEL
- THIN PAPER
- SCISSORS
- ADHESIVE SPRAY
- ETCHING SPRAY

PROJECT FOUR

Decorating a window with an etched pattern

If you have a small bathroom or very little natural light coming in, it is a shame to block the window with curtains or blinds. And when bathrooms are fitted with thick obscuring glass designed to stop the neighbours seeing you in the bath, this is not always very attractive.

In both cases, and with plain glass, the window can be decorated with etching spray. This will allow you to keep clear glass in the top half of the window and stencil a frosted pattern of your own creation on the lower section to give you all the privacy you need.

A window decorated with etching spray is a subtle and attractive way of creating privacy without blocking out the light with curtains or blinds.

HOW TO DO IT

STEP 1 Clean the window and allow it to dry. Fold four strips of paper 30 mm wide and the length and height of the window into a concertina, then cut out a fancy pattern on one edge. Flatten the strips out and lightly apply adhesive spray to one side.

STEP 2 Fold another three strips of paper into 30 mm squares concertina-wise, and draw simple motifs in the middle. Cut these out and spray one side lightly as above.

STEP 3 Stick the borders around the window up to the desired height, and then arrange the motifs across the window pane in a geometric or random pattern. Mask out the surrounding area with paper to protect from the spray.

STEP 4 Spray on a light and even coating of etching spray. You can always apply a second coat if this is too thin and patchy, but it is best to apply one continuous coat first and then leave it to dry. Peel off one of the motifs to check the effect and apply a second coat of etching spray if necessary.

The contemporary bathroom

Big changes have been taking place in the bathroom. It began in new hip hotels where minimalism took over from opulence and before long everyone was at it. This look is the antidote to Victorian and Edwardian repro style, which was the last big style statement for bathrooms. The big thing to note is that fashions take longer to change in bathrooms for the obvious reason that you can't move things around or replace them on a whim. The second factor is cost because this is a room where expert help is definitely required, and plumbers, electricians and builders don't come cheap. If you are going for a complete change then it may be worth asking an architect or specialist bathroom designer to advise you.

The contemporary bathroom replaces opulence with minimalism, giving domestic bathrooms the hip hotel look.

Plumbers and electricians often work together on bathroom installations and it is worth finding a pair who work well as a team. An electric shower, for instance, needs the expertise of a plumber and electrician at different stages. It is also a good idea to consult a plumber before you hire a designer because you need to know what the water pressure is, the type of boiler and size of tank. The plumber will also be able to advise you, for instance, whether it is worth replacing an old boiler at the same time to accommodate a shower system, which would be more economical to run. And if you can find a 'new wave' creative plumber who keeps up with what's new in bathrooms, you won't be needing any other bathroom design advice.

Shop around

The first step is to get hold of as many top class catalogues as you can and make your style choice. Cut out your favourites and prepare to move downmarket in search of look-alikes. As with high street clothes stores there are lots of budget versions of the latest styles, and the DIY outlets should be your first port of call. If you are on a tight budget always go for the plainest designs because they will be the slowest to date.

There is also a booming mail order trade in bathroom fixtures and fittings, and you may be able to economise by getting hold of a plain bath and toilet from a DIY store, making your style statement with accessories and a state-of-the-art sink. Bathroom cabinets, heated towel rails, mirrors, shelves, lights and laundry bins can all be bought in co-ordinating contemporary ranges, and extra items can go on a birthday or Christmas present list!

The best advice is to shop around before you buy because some copies of designer items are as low on quality as they are on price, and it may be worth waiting for a sale of the real thing, or buying last year's range from an outlet. That is particularly true because style changes take a long time to filter down to the cheap end of the market, sometimes taking two or three years.

Planning a brand new bathroom

One of the most important aspects of planning is your budget, and it should include the cost of the main sanitaryware (bath, toilet, bidet, basin, shower tray), the taps, shower, and the screen or cubicle. Also include decorating materials such as tiles, paint, flooring and essential accessories like storage units, lights, towel rails, mirrors and shelves. Get quotes for the plumbing, electrics and carpentry, and any decorating that you can't manage yourself, such as skim coating or replastering. If you add these up and are still smiling skip the next paragraph!

Upgrading your old bathroom

If you like the idea of a new bathroom but not the price, it's time to take stock and take action. If the bathroom suite is outdated or plain ugly it will have to be disguised. Materials to think about are pure white laminated board, perspex or sheet metal. If you like the look of an aluminium bath panel but not its price, then buy a sheet of marine ply and spray it with metallic aluminium spray paint. Spend money on the trim and it will look every bit as good as the real thing. Paint is still the cheapest and most dramatic way to make changes, and you can use it on walls, tiles, woodwork and even vinyl flooring.

Pick a colour scheme with a contemporary feel, something like ice blue, linen white and café latte with accents of dull silver. Box in the bath and basin with ply, paint the walls ice blue and linen white, paint the floor café latte and fit matching coloured blinds. Then change the toilet seat, shower curtain, bath mat, loo roll holder,

PAINTING TILES AND FLOORS

In the 1990s, interior designers' quest for originality meant that products on the industrial side were taken up by the home sector. Non-slip floor paints were one of the first products to cross over from the factories and shipyards, and many other resurfacing products and specialised finishes followed. The next four projects show how to transform three shiny bathroom surfaces: tiles are primed and painted, vinyl flooring is given a whole new look, and a window is decorated with etching spray.

towel rail and mirror. This doesn't necessarily mean buy everything new – keep a look out for things that can be transformed with paint, like woven laundry baskets or mirror frames. Galvanised metal is very cheap and has been taken up by some contemporary designers for mirror frames, candle holders and small cupboards. Classic items like buckets and utility shelving can be bought from hardware stores and integrated with designer buys. In short, this is the sort of quick fix that you can do in a weekend. So what on earth are you waiting for?

Designer catalogues can help you decide on the look you want, before looking for a budget version in DIY outlets. Sometimes it's worth waiting for a sale of the real thing to prevent sacrificing quality for price.

YOU WILL NEED:
• SUGAR SOAP OR WALL
  AND FLOOR CLEANER
• SCOURING SPONGE
• OLD TOWEL
• TILE PRIMER
• SMALL FOAM ROLLER
  AND TRAY
• MASKING TAPE
• GLOSS OR EGGSHELL
  PAINT IN CHOSEN
  COLOUR
• EXTRA ROLLER

PROJECT ONE

Painting tiles

This is one of those miracles where doing and seeing what you've done is believing.

NOTE

If you want the tiles to look convincingly ceramic, then scrape out the old grout before you paint and re-grout the tiles afterwards, following the steps shown in the tile grouting project.

HOW TO DO IT

STEP 1 Wash down the tiled area, and dry it well with an old towel to get rid of any surface water. Mask off the edges of the tiled area with masking tape, and then pour some of the tile primer into the tray and apply a thin, even coat with the small foam roller. Leave to dry. If the tile pattern or colour shows through, then apply one more coat. Clean the tray and fit a new roller.

STEP 2 Pour the feature colour paint into the tray and use the roller to apply it to the tiles. Leave to dry and then apply a second coat.

Old tiles can be transformed into ceramic look-alikes with a coat of tile primer and a coat of gloss.

YOU WILL NEED:
- VINYL FLAIR FLOOR PAINT (1 LTR COVERS 15SQ M)
- SUGAR SOAP
- LARGE SPONGE
- BUCKET
- SMALL HIGH DENSITY SPONGE ROLLER AND TRAY

Transform those hated vinyl floor patterns with a couple of coats of paint. Try to allow a few days for it to dry, to make it last longer.

Painting a vinyl floor

This may seem like a very lazy option but don't knock it if it works! Vinyl flooring is the most practical and comfortable flooring for a bathroom, but some of the patterns really let the material down. Until recently the only options were to live with it or rip it out and fit new flooring, but there is now a third option, and that is paint. It is much cheaper and far less hassle to use than cutting out templates and replacing something that's practical, and in good condition, because you loathe the colour or pattern. The paint is a specialist type, but it is now available from several major DIY outlets.

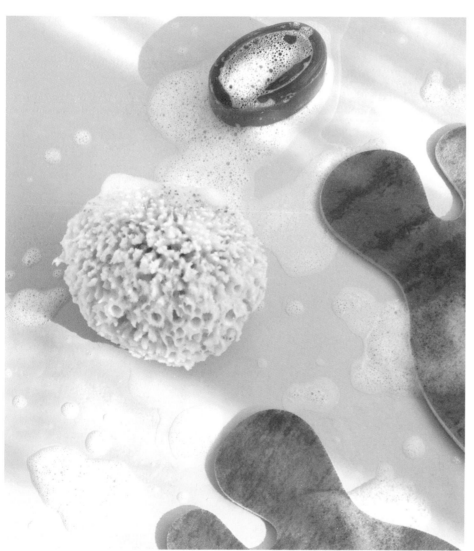

HOW TO DO IT

STEP 1 Before you begin painting, the floor must be spotlessly clean. Fill a bucket with hot water and dissolve the sugar soap as directed. Clean the floor and leave it to dry.

STEP 2 Apply the paint with the roller. Do not apply it too thickly because it will develop an unpleasant film. If, however, you apply it too thinly it will wear off. For the best results, apply two to three even coats for a thorough covering. The first coat should be touch dry in an hour and the second coat can be applied in 4 hours time. The paint can be walked on after 6 hours but will be even tougher if you leave it for a few days. It will provide a long-lasting finish.

YOU WILL NEED:

- **COLOURED GROUTING IN A COLOUR OF YOUR CHOICE**
- **SCRAPER OR SMALL SCREWDRIVER TO CLEAN OUT OLD GROUT**
- **SPONGE WITH SCOURER**
- **FLEXIBLE GROUT SPREADER**
- **GROUT SHAPER (ROUND ENDED)**
- **SOFT DRY CLOTH**

PROJECT THREE

Coloured grouting

Grout is the filler between tiles, which can be used decoratively to make a very obvious grid of coloured lines. It comes in a good range of colours and is easy to apply.

The finishing touches to freshly painted tiles, or simply to freshen up existing tiles, coloured grouting is an easy way to give your tiles a new look.

HOW TO DO IT

STEP 1 Run the grout scraper (or another suitable tool) along the old grout and scrape most of it away. Don't allow the scraper to skid across the tiles and damage the surface, or to dig too deep and affect the tile adhesive.

STEP 2 Dampen the scouring sponge and run it down the scraped gaps between the tiles to remove any loose material.

STEP 3 Use a flexible spreader to press the grout into the gaps so that there are no air bubbles left.

STEP 4 Next, use the sponge to wipe away any excess grout from the tiles and use a shaping tool to mould the grout into a slightly concave shape. Wipe away any smears, leave to dry, and finally polish the tiles with a dry, soft cloth.

YOU WILL NEED:

- DE-GREASING WINDOW CLEANING SPRAY AND CLOTH
- ETCHING SPRAY
- MASKING TAPE
- TAPE MEASURE OR RULER
- PLAIN PAPER
- ADHESIVE SPRAY

PROJECT FOUR

Decorating a window with etching spray

This gives a cool contemporary look to a bathroom window, and obscures the view from outside. The design is more of a style statement, and the spray could also be used to make a matching border for a bathroom mirror. The same spray is used for a project in the traditional bathroom, so just follow the steps for the method.

Decorating a window with etching spray gains privacy without curtains or blinds while adding a cool, contemporary look. Your own design would do just as well as the one shown.

HOW TO DO IT

STEP 1 Run a frame of masking tape 20 mm inside the edge of the window, attaching paper to protect the surrounding area.

STEP 2 Enlarge the h_2o on a photocopier to fill an A4 sheet, then cut them out and apply adhesive spray to the back. Place the letters inside the masked frame and then frost the window with the etching spray. Peel off the tape and the templates.

Shower room

A home with a bathroom and separate shower room has the best of both worlds, allowing you to freshen up quickly or relax and enjoy a long soak in warm bubbles. Ensuite bathrooms are often shower rooms through lack of space. But even if space is not an issue, if you really prefer a shower to a bath anytime, it could make sense to get rid of the bath altogether and enjoy the luxury of a spacious shower room instead. And if, at a later date, you decide you do want a bath, one can simply be put in.

You can now find showers small enough to fit into almost any space, so cupboards become potential shower rooms.

In a small flat a shower is more economical space-wise, and is also a good option as an en suite facility for teenagers. This idea could save many a row over how long certain people spend in the bathroom! However, babies and very small children usually hate showers and getting water in their eyes, and washing their hair under an overhead shower can be a nightmare, so stick to the sink for that job. Or try an adjustable shower which you can set at the right height so you don't splash water in their faces, which is what tends to cause all the fuss.

A range of possibilities

If you are starting a shower room from scratch, it is worth considering doing without a cubicle and tray and instead turning the whole room into a walk-in shower. You will need the help of a plumber, electrician and carpenter. The shower fittings are fixed on the wall, and the floor will have to be raised slightly to create a slope to a central drain. The shower room can then be tiled, grouted and silicone sealed. Slatted wooden boards are also a good idea on part of the floor, to prevent slipping and minimise puddles. The luxury of a shower room like this could actually cost less than buying a new tray and cubicle.

If you are fitting a cubicle, tray and shower in a small room that doesn't have a toilet or basin, try not to clutter it up too much because space is one of the biggest luxuries in a shower room. Walls only need to be tiled outside the shower unit if it doesn't have glass on all sides, so the rest of the room can be decorated for comfort and convenience. Have a rail to warm towels over the radiator, or replace the radiator with a large heated towel rail. A bathroom cupboard, shelf and a mirror with good lighting are the other essentials. If the room is small and square this might also be a good place to fit a false ceiling with recessed lights fitted with a dimmer switch, operated from outside the shower room. All lighting should be of the sealed-unit type suitable for bathrooms. And also make sure there is some ventilation because steam needs to escape if you are to avoid condensation problems.

Adaptability

Shower manufacturers boast of making units that can fit into almost any space, and that can mean somewhere as small as a cupboard. And with new combination boilers, water is heated on demand without the need for a large hot water storage tank in an airing cupboard. So if you are changing the boiler why not investigate the possibility of fitting a new shower? Who knows, your airing cupboard may just be big enough for a shower with a folding door. Another good shower option is having one near the back door. This is especially useful if you live near the beach, on a farm, or

have an occupation or play a sport that means you return home grubby and sweaty. It is also an ideal place for kids to be sluiced down as they come in from the garden. This is a no-frills sort of shower, with rendered and tiled stud walls and a heavy-duty PVC shower curtain on a rail. Fit a mirror, and soap and shampoo tray inside and have a handy towel hook outside with a wooden duckboard to step out onto.

En suite shower room

An en suite shower room must be waterproof, warm and welcoming. Privacy comes with the territory and you can afford to think more about the design and less about the barricading. Flexible MDF wood is a relatively new material that makes building curves possible. This could be used to create the base for a curved mosaic wall instead of a glass shower cubicle. Mosaic

tiles can be bought and applied in sheets, which makes tiling curves easier than you would imagine. Mosaics come in many other colours than 'swimming pool' blue, and while you're at it, why not try your hand at a mirror frame or simple frieze? Be warned though, the mosaic habit is a difficult one to kick. The best floor treatment for a shower room like this would be tiles or sheet vinyl, but do make sure that you always step onto a dry bath mat to avoid wet feet on the bedroom carpet.

If the en suite is for a teenager make sure that there are plenty of hooks to hang up towels, and a radiator to dry the bath mat on. One day they'll realise that towels and bath mats are revolting if they stay on the floor in a wet heap! It is also vital to make sure that the shower is totally watertight, and it may even be worth building a low tiled wall that you step over at the entrance to the room. It is better to anticipate problems now than deal with them later.

There is one element to showering that hasn't really been mentioned, and that is the pleasure to be had from standing under a powerful stream of warm water. A power shower option is a really good idea for those times when you need kick-starting in the morning or when you need a blast to unwind you after work. Ask your plumber about a power-shower pump unit, which can be switched on and off from outside the bathroom. This will allow you to conserve hot water and electricity when an ordinary shower will do, and will give you the option of having an exhilarating power shower when you really need it.

THE PROJECTS
The main issues facing you when decorating a shower room are what to do about the walls and floor. The following projects offer some ideas.

(Left) Only the inside walls of a shower cubicle need tiling. The other walls can be decorated with paint.

A refreshing wake-up shower in an ensuite shower room is a perfect morning tonic, especially if you add the exhilaration of a power shower.

YOU WILL NEED:
- 8 x 70-mm LENGTHS OF 50-mm x 25-mm PAR PINE
- 2 x 45-mm LENGTHS OF 50-mm x 25-mm PAR PINE
- TENON SAW
- MEDIUM AND FINE SANDPAPER
- COMBINATION SQUARE
- DRILL WITH COUNTERSINK BIT AND 6-mm BIT
- 16 x 60-mm No. 6 COUNTERSINK SCREWS (NON-RUSTING)
- WOODSTAIN, CLEAR VARNISH OR WAX
- BRUSH

PROJECT ONE

A pine duckboard

S ay goodbye to soggy bathmats or standing in a puddle on a wet floor by making yourself this little deck to stand on when you get out of the shower. This duckboard is made from pine softwood, which is very easy to cut. The lengths can be sanded smooth and coloured with an exterior quality woodstain or just varnished to seal the surface.

This practical and stylish duckboard is easy to make from pine softwood, and finished with either wood stain or simply varnished.

HOW TO DO IT

STEP 1 Cut all the lengths of timber then sand any sharp edges to round them off slightly. Pay particular attention to the sawn ends.

STEP 2 Line the lengths up and mark the positions for the two cross-pieces.

STEP 3 Drill a countersunk clearance hole for a screw at each end of all the lengths and screw the lengths to the cross-pieces.

STEP 4 Stain, wax or simply varnish the duckboard. Apply the wax with a soft, lint-free cloth, leave to dry for 20 minutes, then buff with wire wool.

PROJECT TWO

A customised shower curtain

Plastic shower curtains aren't the most attractive sight in a shower room, but only one side of the shower curtain needs to be water-repellent, so why not use a cheap plastic curtain trimmings as the lining for something more in keeping with your own bathroom style? The curtain is only fixed to the liner at the top, above the level where it will come into contact with any water, so the stitch perforations will not be a problem. Any lightweight fabric which is not too prone to creasing is suitable for this project and the decorative additions are up to you. The daisies can be stuck to the fabric with a good fabric glue, or hand-stitched if you prefer.

Practical plastic shower curtains can be made into attractive versions with just a covering of fabric, a choice of decorations and a sewing machine.

HOW TO DO IT

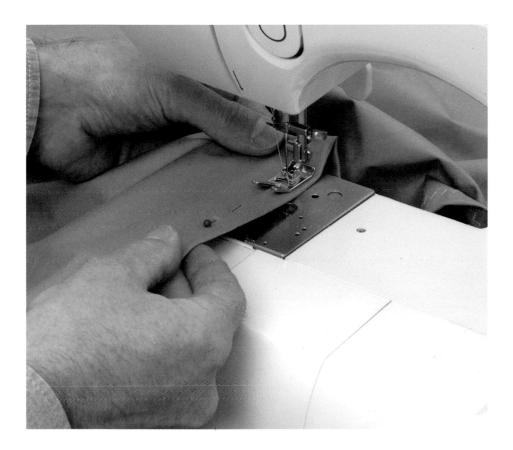

STEP 1 If the fabric is too wide, then cut it and hem it to match the size of the shower curtain. Measure the length against the shower curtain and sew a small hem at the top and bottom.

STEP 2 Line up the top of the cotton curtain with the top of the plastic curtain. Stitch the two together just below the holes for the shower rings. Use matching thread so that the stitches are invisible.

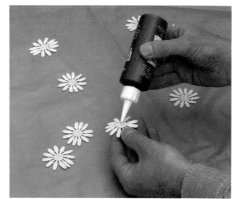

STEP 3 Arrange the daisies all over the curtain in a random 'natural' lawn pattern. Stick them onto the fabric with the fabric glue and leave until it has dried and bonded. If you prefer they can be slipstitched in place.

YOU WILL NEED:
- A NICE PLANK OF WOOD, ABOUT 500 MM X 100 MM. DRIFTWOOD IS IDEAL BUT NEW WOOD WITH AN INTERESTING GRAIN, SUCH AS AN OFF-CUT OF PARANÁ PINE OR A FRUIT WOOD, WOULD ALSO LOOK GOOD. ASK A TIMBER MERCHANT WHAT SUITABLE OFF-CUTS THEY HAVE, EXPLAINING THE USE IT WILL BE PUT TO. YOU MAY ALSO LIKE TO STAIN AND VARNISH THE WOOD.
- SOAP DISH
- 2 HOOKS
- DRILL
- 10-MM TILE BIT
- MASKING TAPE
- MARKER PEN
- SPIRIT LEVEL
- NON-RUSTING SCREWS TO ATTACH THE HOOKS (MOST COME WITH SCREWS)
- 2 x 75-MM No. 10 SCREWS TO FIX THE WOOD TO THE TILED WALL (THE SCREW LENGTH
- DEPENDS UPON THE DEPTH OF YOUR WOOD)
- WALL PLUGS
- BRASS CUPPED SCREWS
- BRADAWL

PROJECT THREE

Shower caddy

Trying to locate the soap, shampoo or sponge can be highly frustrating when water is cascading into your eyes. This simple solution should help to keep everything you need in one place, close to hand when you need it. It is ideally suited to a tiled wall and its beauty lies in the fact that only two holes are drilled through the tiling, with the rest going into the wooden support.

This shower caddy lets you have a range of fittings with only two holes drilled through the tiles. All the rest are drilled to the wooden caddy.

HOW TO DO IT

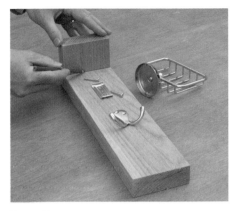

STEP 1 Find the ideal position for the caddy on the shower wall, making quite sure that there are no pipes behind the tiles where the screws will be located! Mark the positions for the components and the shelf.

STEP 2 Drill two evenly spaced holes in the shelf end.

STEP 3 Screw the top shelf to the back plank using brass cupped screws. Screw the hooks and soap dish into position.

STEP 4 Place the unit in position on the wall. Mark through the pre-drilled holes onto the wall using a bradawl.

STEP 5 Drill holes through the tiles using a tile bit. Plug the wall.

STEP 6 Screw the unit to the wall using the brass cupped screws.

Fun & study

Working from home is many people's dream – no traffic jams, no train delays, no office politics. But whether you're going to be working from home full-time or just a few hours a week, your work area needs to be carefully planned so that you can switch from a domestic to a work environment without one intruding on the other. Home offices are also an opportunity to have fun with design – at last you don't have to put up with grey metal filing cabinets because your office is to suit you, and you alone. This section shows how to create stylish working spaces, either in separate offices or in part of a living area. It also looks at creating a teenager's study and a child's playroom.

Office-living space

The keyword in home office design is flexibility and nowhere more so than in a room that serves several purposes. Ideally you want to be able to put away the working day without a trace of it left in the evening, and to start again effortlessly the next morning. This might seem like a tall order but with so many of us choosing to work from home there is a wealth of design expertise in this area. It is now possible to buy fantastic pieces of furniture which look like stylish wardrobes, sideboards or bookshelves at night but which open out into a full working office during the day. They have been designed so that a full desk with computers, bookshelves and files can be closed without putting anything away. Wonders like this don't come cheap, but when you consider the cost of renting and fitting out an office it puts the price into perspective.

Despite the age of the computer, a fair amount of paperwork means old-fashioned filing systems are not quite dead. If your home office is also your living room, it's worth making your filing system as attractive as possible.

If your office is to be at one end of the living room, a divider of some sort will allow the room to be used for both purposes at the same time. Modular cubed units are excellent for this, especially if you have a mixture of some open cubes and others with doors. Mix the cubes so that some face the office and some the living room. If you prefer something less solid then a screen is the best idea. There are lots of different styles in the shops and catalogues including minimalist Japanese, decoratively carved Indian style, wrought iron, and bamboo and seagrass. Screens are not difficult to make and the basic construction technique described in the Traditional Living Room section could be used to make a larger office screen. Another option is to fit a Venetian blind. It will add a sharp, efficient look to the office and you can vary the level of exclusion from the rest of the room by adjusting the slats. At the end of the working day you have the option of lowering and closing it to block the view of the office.

It is a good idea to have your office equipment, including the desk, on castors. This allows you maximum flexibility because everything can be easily moved around or out of the room altogether if the occasion demands. A wall-mounted cupboard with sliding doors will look good and conceal loads of files, catalogues and magazines, and a low sideboard is a perfect piece of dual-purpose furniture. If you have a dining room you could use a dining table as your daytime desk and a sideboard for storing all your paperwork without anyone being any the wiser. It is only viable for tidy, organised people with very good memories.

The Essentials

Top of the list is some sort of work surface that may be a proper desk or a table with a drawer unit. Begin by making a realistic list of all the things you will need in your home office and if you use a computer allow plenty of space for all the extra bits and pieces like zip drives, scanners and printers. Several stylish mail order companies have ranges of contemporary desk units with all the proper shelves, including a low keyboard shelf which is advisable if you going to be using the computer everyday. Ideally the monitor should be at eye level and your arms should be level with the keyboard. Desks don't have to cost much at all, in fact they are often given away free when you buy a new computer. A pair of trestles topped with a piece of MDF will also make a great desk, especially if you invest in one or two filing cabinets and drawer units on castors, which can be wheeled out of sight when the office is shut. A proper office chair is essential for anyone spending more than an hour a day sitting at a desk. Aim to spend as much money as you can on the chair and economise elsewhere. To avoid backache and repetitive stress injury (RSI), which causes pain in your fingers and wrists, you should sit with a straight back, your feet flat on the floor and elbows at your side as you tap the keyboard.

Organisation

If your working area also serves another purpose, it is more important than ever to be really well organised. Computers were supposed to take the place of paperwork but that hasn't completely happened yet, and most of us find that we still need an old-fashioned filing system. Then there are pens, pencils, rulers, paper clips, stationery and all the bits and bobs relevant to your work. A strong set of shelves for reference books, box files and magazines could be fitted with a blind to hide them when you're not working. And a smart set of matching boxes to keep on display is particularly useful for clearing away all your clutter at the end of each working day. A notice board and calendar are also essential if you are to keep track of appointments, and there are some excellent programmes for the computer which act as Post-It notes and daily, weekly and monthly diary pages.

THE PROJECTS
The project on the following pages is the ultimate in flexibility, allowing you to keep the clutter of a desk in organised compartments, which can be put away after use.

Lighting

The best light to work by is a directional light, angled to illuminate your desk area. In addition the room needs either good natural light, or artificial ambient light, for the evening or dull days so that the contrast between the brightness of a computer screen and the rest of the room is never too great. Use overhead or wall lights to balance the lighting.

Pleasing yourself

One of the joys of working from home is that your office need not bear any resemblance to an office at all. So, be creative and remember that this is home first and an office second. A large wicker hamper is as good as a metal cupboard for keeping box files in, and polka-dotted tumblers can hold pencils and paper clips. Biscuit barrels hold several rolls of tape and balls of string, and a CD storage rack takes care of the CD Roms and zip disks. A typist's chair can be re-covered to match the curtains, a vase of flowers will do more for the desk top than any executive toy, and when the day's work is done why not treat your computer like a birdcage and cover it with a large silk scarf.

A home office doesn't have to look like an office at all. Wicker hampers with compartments serve as useful storage space and you can never go wrong with a vase of fresh flowers.

YOU WILL NEED:
• A SHEET OF 19-MM
   MDF CUT AS
   FOLLOWS:
BACK 62 CM X
   89 CM
TOP SHELF 30 CM X
   89 CM
BOTTOM SHELF 25 CM
   X 30 CM
SMALL SIDE SHELVES
   15-CM X 15-CM
   (2 PIECES)
LEFT-HAND SIDE
   62 CM X 66 CM
RIGHT-HAND SIDE
   62 CM X 20 CM
LEFT UPRIGHTS 45-CM X
   30-CM (2 PIECES)
RIGHT UPRIGHTS 45-CM
   X 15-CM (2 PIECES)
• No. 6 38-MM SCREWS
• WOOD GLUE
• WORKBENCH
• JIGSAW
• TAPE MEASURE
• COMBINATION
   SQUARE
• CARPENTER'S PENCIL
• DRILL WITH PILOT,
   SCREW AND
   COUNTERSINK BIT
   (USE SIZE 4
   SCREWSINK BIT FOR
   ALL THREE)
• LONG RULE
• SANDPAPER

PROJECT ONE
A desktop unit

The work surface can be a table or simply a sheet of thick board supported on a pair of trestles, but what turns it into an efficient desk are the drawer units, shelves and storage space. This project shows how to build a free-standing unit to sit on top of the work surface. It includes space for the computer monitor, storage for CD Roms and discs, two file compartments, a stationery tray compartment and a book-ended shelf on the top.

When this desktop unit is sat on a table it creates an instant work surface. It keeps all your desktop clutter in an organised space, which can be quickly put away after use.

HOW TO DO IT

STEP 1 Hold the uprights, dividers and shelves against the back section and mark out their positions in pencil on the back.

STEP 2 Draw, cut and sand the mitred corners on the two sides.

STEP 3 Measure and draw a 15-cm-square box at the bottom of the central section on the back piece. This will be cut out to serve as a channel for the computer cables.

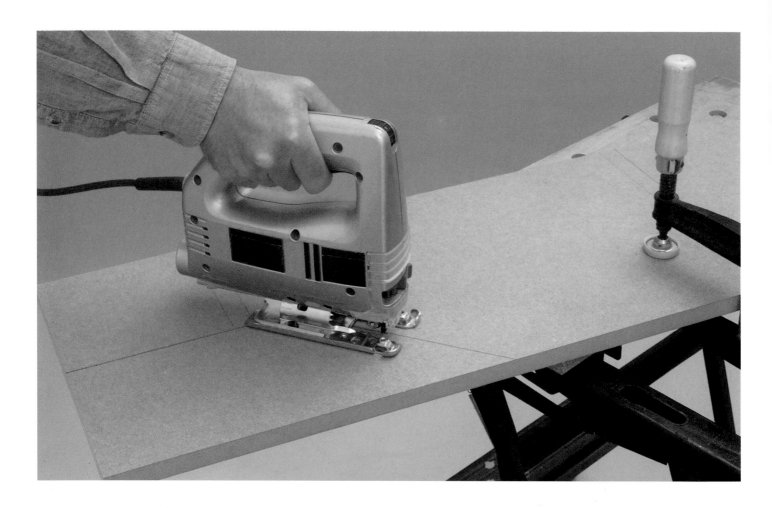

STEP 4 Use a jigsaw to cut out the cable box and the top shelf shape.

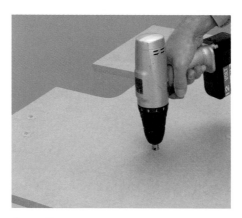

STEP 5 Drill clearance holes on the back section and countersink.

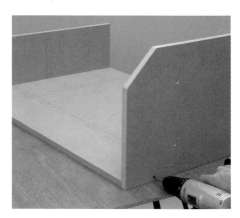

STEP 6 Fix the uprights to the back section.

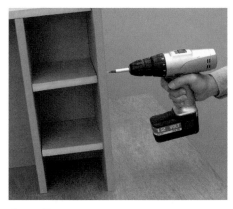

STEP 7 Fix the sides to the two uprights. Fix the smaller shelves to the sides and back.

STEP 8 Fill the holes, sand, and paint in your chosen colour.

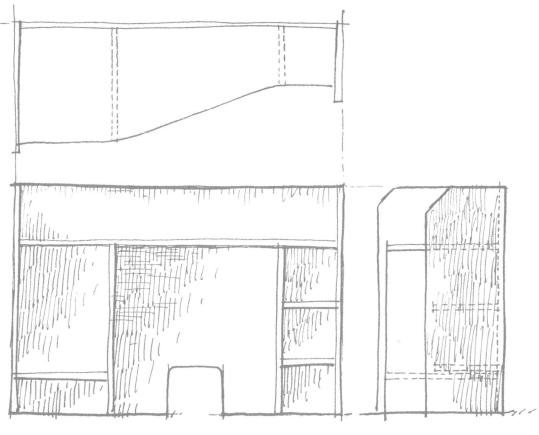

Use this sketch to help you construct your desk. Remember to measure all the timber accurately and use a spirit level to ensure that everything is level.

Home office

Computers have revolutionised our world to the point where many more of us now work from home. Why spend time commuting to and from the office when everything can be done here and not there? And if that's the route you are taking, it really is worth designing and decorating your new office.

The first thing you need to do when planning a new office in your home is decide what you will use it for, for how often and what equipment you will need to keep in it. Then you can look at what you would like in your home office, as well as what you will need. As the boss, you're in the lucky position of making all the decisions, so don't feel constrained by any preconceived ideas of how an office should or shouldn't look. Six things to consider when planning your home office are...

When space is at a premium, or you only plan to work at home part-time, an area underneath the staircase can be an ideal working space.

Location

A spare bedroom or a dining room are the rooms most likely to be turned into an office, but when space is at a premium you could make use of a landing or even a cupboard under the stairs. A lot depends upon how many of you share the home – if you're on your own or a couple it will be a lot easier to set the office boundaries than if you have a family. Working from home with young children is not impossible, but it is a challenge.

If you have an attic, garage or outhouse with conversion potential then it is worth finding out what it will cost. If you plan to work from home in the long term, then an office slightly removed from the home environment could be the perfect solution. If you are only planning to work a few hours a day though, then you could make do with a very small but highly organised work area, and the space under the stairs is not as funny as it sounds. The idea is not to disappear into a cupboard and close the door behind you, but to think of your office as part of an open-plan design. The best scenario is where the stairs run up the side of the room. Your desk, storage, filing and bookshelves can be tucked into the space underneath the staircase while you actually sit in the room facing it, without being claustrophobic!

If you are at work in complete isolation, then arrange everything to suit yourself, but if you expect to see visitors then the office should be as close to the front door as possible to minimise domestic intrusion. Maintaining a professional attitude is difficult enough at home without having strangers peering at your unmade beds and unwashed breakfast plates.

Electricity

One of the first things to consider is do you need more electric and phone sockets? The fax and internet connections are best on a separate line so that they don't interfere with the home phone number. In fact new phone line options are being introduced all the time, so seek advice from your phone company. With sockets, the basic strips can take four plugs, but you can also buy a more expensive version with eight sockets and two phone sockets. Be generous with your socket allowance so that you avoid trailing cables in the work area. Computers should also be plugged into surge protectors, which block destructive power surges during electrical storms. Plan your lighting at this stage too, so that your work area is well lit and the rest of the room has a pleasant ambient lighting system. Having a good background light level prevents eye strain from a bright computer screen. Daylight bulbs mimic natural light and are reputed to be easier on the eyes, and getting the lighting right keeps you alert and prevents tiredness.

Fitting and furnishing

A flick through an office supplier's catalogue will show you that there isn't just a gadget for everything, but different versions of each gadget. So be assured that whatever your special office needs, they can be met. And if it's just a desk, chair and filing cabinet that you're after, they also come in a huge range of styles and prices.

Spend as much money as you can afford on a good adjustable chair, one that assures you of having the right posture when you're working.

Ideally your back should be straight with the lumbar region of your spine well supported, thighs parallel to the floor and both feet flat on the ground. This may mean having a raised foot rest under your feet if you are not working at an ergonomically designed computer desk. To find out what the correct posture feels like, simply place a few books under your feet and a rolled towel in the small of your back.

Fully adjustable office chairs have levers for tilting and altering the seat and back support height. Since they can be very expensive it really is worth looking in a second-hand office supplies shop. And because businesses regularly close down or have a change in office style, second hand does not necessarily mean worn out. Filing cabinets, letter trays and drawer units are other potentially expensive items that can be bought second-hand and given a make-over to match your home-office style. In fact these stores can be

A good adjustable office chair is one item of furniture you cannot afford to be without. Second-hand chairs can be just as good as new, so it doesn't need to break the bank.

White looks good with everything and is a colour that won't distract you from your work. A floating laminated floor is another plain colour and a material that works well with chairs on castors.

real Aladdin's caves, and you never know what you'll find. There is no need to surround yourself with dull utilitarian grey or beige metal cabinets just because they are the only colours on offer. Buy the poor dull things and inject a bit of fun by giving them an uplifting colour change with metal primer and enamel paints from a car accessory store. If meetings or interviews are part of your work then you will also need to provide seating for your visitors. A lot depends on your line of work, and if it is quite buzzy and informal then stools would be fine, otherwise consider a smart compact sofa bed and then you will even be able to offer friends a bed for the night!

Walls

Decorating the home office should encourage you to spend time in there without any distractions. One of the most difficult aspects of working from home is being able to disengage yourself from any domestic jobs that need doing. The very last thing you need is to be constantly looking round and thinking that the room could do with a good coat of paint and a new set of curtains. Concentrate on work. You haven't time for all that! Get the decorating done after the electrics and before the arrival of heavy desks and cupboards. Keep the style simple and wall colours light to make the most of the daylight, and don't be afraid to use white, which looks good with everything. Light colours expand spaces and prevent the office from looking crowded once all the equipment is in place.

Windows

When choosing a window treatment for your office it is quite important to choose something that won't look out of place with the rest of your home when seen from the outside. Slatted blinds are the most versatile option because they can be adjusted to admit maximum daylight, filter bright sunlight and block views giving good security. They also look cool and contemporary. Vertical blinds are being used a lot more in homes these days and they do a similar job but with broader vertical slats.

Floors

When it comes to flooring you have the choice of a carpet or hard surface. As ever your choice must be guided by your kind of work. Vinyl or lino is the most hardwearing and easy to clean, and it also has the advantage over carpet when castors are being used. Cork is an inexpensive natural material which is coming back into fashion, particularly the dark stained version. The other hard flooring option is a laminated floating floor. It comes in different quality grades and two basic

designs. Both follow the tongue and groove style with one type needing glue to join the planks, and the other using an interlocking design. The second type can be lifted and moved. If you choose carpet it is a good idea to buy a clear plastic chair mat which will allow you to move and swivel easily around your desk area.

PROJECTS

The three projects on the following pages focus on three essential parts of any home office: lighting, storage and, of course, the desk space. But to make the most of the freedom allowed by the home office, the emphasis is on fun as well as function, allowing a bit of creativity to be added to the work environment. A fresh coat of paint, a little disciplined filing and a big vase of flowers should do the rest.

Wardrobes can be made into stationery cupboards or complete workstations. At the end of the day, the doors can be closed on anything resembling work.

You will need:
- 100 -mm x 25-mm timber for box frame
- Adhesive
- Thin Perspex for front
- 12-mm MDF for base
- Drill
- Fluorescent striplight to fit the box size
- Arrow shape cut out of card
- Scalpel
- Adhesive spray
- 2 mirror fixings
- Right-angled moulding
- Spray glue

PROJECT ONE
Lighting

If you are converting a bedroom or dining room into an office, the chances are that you will have to completely rethink the lighting. The two types of lighting needed are ambient, which is the background lighting all around you, and task lighting, which is directional lighting illuminating your work area. If you also have a seating area for clients this could be lit from above with a pendant lamp. This project shows how to light an office area.

We are all familiar with light boxes, usually with the message EXIT on them. This project is a bit of fun along these lines. Use two dark-coloured pieces of cardboard cut in arrow shapes, which will show through the Perspex. The glass is then assembled in a box frame with a fluorescent tube inside.

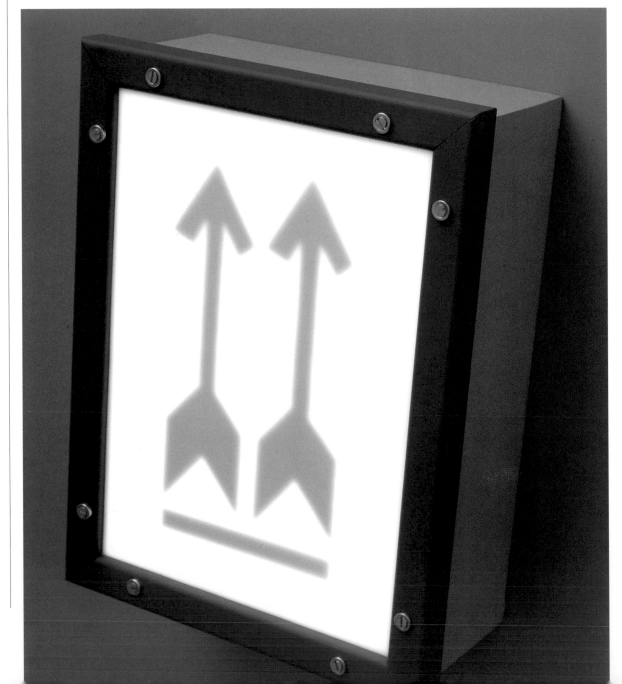

An exit sign with a difference! This novel light box uses Perspex in front of a fluorescent light tube. You can design your own pattern or lettering for a personal touch.

HOW TO DO IT

STEP 1 Have the white Perspex cut to size, and then cut the wood to size and sand the edges. Make a simple butt-jointed box, glue and screw the joints.

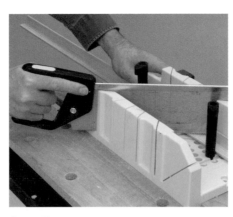

STEP 2 Cut out the right-angle moulding, using a tenon saw and mitring block.

STEP 3 Place the Perspex on top of the box. Drill clearance holes through the moulding and screw it to the Perspex and the box frame.

STEP 4 Cut out the arrow shapes. Spray glue onto the back and stick to the Perspex in the inside of the box.

STEP 5 Drill an exit hole for the cable in the back or the side of the box, and place the fitting and bulb inside the box.

STEP 6 Screw the back of the box in place, add the bulb and fixings and attach to the wall. Paint if desired.

TIP
* You can use any motif or word in your light box – just choose something that is personal to you.

YOU WILL NEED:

• 1 SHEET OF
  18-MM MDF
• LONG RULER
• TAPE MEASURE
• COMBINATION
  SQUARE
• PENCIL
• DRILL
• PILOT BIT AND
  COUNTERSINK BIT
• SCREWS

PROJECT TWO

Storage

There is no getting away from storage. Whatever type of work you do, paperwork mounts up, records must be kept and we all need somewhere to keep telephone directories and reference material. This storage unit on castors will take care of books, files and catalogues. The top is at desk height, so with a piece of MDF laid on top it provides an extra work surface.

This handy storage unit on castors keeps books, files and catalogues accessible at the same time as neatly stored away. An optional top surface of MDF will make an additional work surface.

HOW TO DO IT

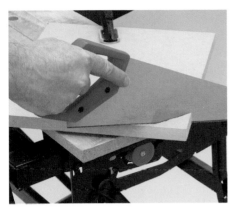

STEP 1 Cut the back of the unit from the sheet of MDF. It should be the height of your desk minus the height of the castors if you want to extend the desk area. Cut out all the shelves, dividers and the top, sides and bottom of the unit.

STEP 2 Draw the positions of the sides, top and bottom, and all the partitions and shelves in pencil on the back. Use a length of MDF to do this so that you can see a flat plan of the unit on the back.

STEP 3 Drill clearance holes to fix all the pieces to the back of the unit. Hold each piece in position as you drill through the clearance holes to make pilot holes for the screws.

STEP 4 Assemble the outer frame first, applying wood glue to the joining edges before screwing them together through the back. Drill pilot, clearance and countersink holes, then secure the corner joints by screwing them together. Fit all the partitions in place first, and then add the shelves. Drill, glue and screw each one so that the whole unit stands firm.

STEP 5 Finally drill holes and fit the four castors onto the base of the unit.

STEP 6 Sand all the sharp edges smooth, then paint if required, or use it just as it is.

PROJECT THREE

Curved desk

Y ou can make a very smart desk from one sheet of MDF and a pair of trestles. Or you can buy the legs in sets of four, as shown in this project, which are then simply attached to the underside of the desk. This desk is ideal for someone whose desk is always piled high because it is shaped like a curve, so when you sit at it, everything is within arm's reach.

A simple curved desk made out of MDF is both stylish and functional. You can either buy a pair of trestles or four, ready-made legs.

HOW TO DO IT

STEP 1 Support the MDF between two saw horses or trestles. Draw the curve in pencil, either from the pattern or to your own plan. Cut out the curve with a jigsaw and sand.

STEP 2 Support the desk leg in the work bench and drill a vertical hole for fitting.

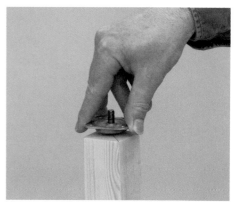

STEP 3 The leg fittings consist of two parts – one post with a screw fitting to fit into the leg and one to receive the post which fits under the table top.

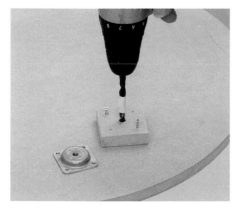

STEP 4 Screw the squares of timber to the underneath of the table, then mark the positions for the legs and all their screws. Drill pilot holes using a 2-mm drill bit.

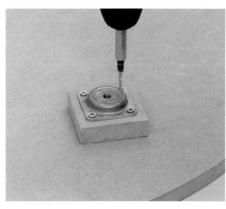

STEP 5 Screw the top receiving plate of the leg fitting into the timber boss.

STEP 6 Screw each leg into position. Lift the table and turn. Seal the surfaces with MDF primer or a 50:50 dilution of PVA and water. Paint or stain and varnish the desk.

TIP
* These table legs are sold in packs in DIY stores, and always have instructions included with them. If you prefer, you could use trestle table legs, which can also be found in DIY stores.

Teenager's study

Creating an environment to encourage a teenage to study is an interesting challenge, and one solution is to put the emphasis on relaxation, keeping a corner that is conducive to study. The best way to do this is to build in a worktop with all the shelving, drawers and electrical sockets that the teenager will need for computers, CDs and video games. There is little point in excluding these things because the object is to get children to spend time in the room and make studying easier. Exclusion simply makes forbidden fruit taste sweeter.

The great thing about the DIY boom is that there is a close link between fashion and decorating styles, with top clothes designers also designing home furnishing ranges. This means that teenagers today are far more conscious of interior design fashions than most of us were at their age. The key to success lies in parent and child working together as a team, doing everything from planning and shopping to actually making the changes. Sometimes as parents we think it is easier to get on and do the work ourselves, but if we do that we are denying our kids the satisfaction of

The best studies for teenagers are those that also include an element of relaxation and entertainment, to entice them into the work area.

working hard and joining in. Begin by asking for a wish list of everything they would have if money were no object, then set a budget and help to edit what is on the list. Try to include an extravagance or two like a fake fur beanbag or a really cool angle-poise lamp. Discuss colour, furniture, lighting and flooring, and look at as many style magazines as you can find. Keep a look out for special features flagged on the front of home magazines, and buy any for home offices, studies or bedsits. If your teenager is likely to go to college then this room could build a bridge between their childhood and future independence.

Practicalities

If you are giving this room a make-over together it is important that the whole process doesn't drag on too long, so stick to a time limit. Paint the walls one weekend, and hire an electrician to fit extra plugs and sort out the lighting at the same time. When it comes to the flooring the best tip is to use expensive underlay and cheap carpeting. The underlay will cut the noise level dramatically, and the carpet can be replaced once your fledgling has flown the nest. A tough cord carpet can always be softened by a large rug for lounging on.

Once the carpet is down the workstation can be built. It should be custom made to meet your teenager's specific needs. Drawer units on castors are a good idea because they allow for more

flexibility. And make the desktop wide and long enough with ample shelving for magazines and reference books, with smaller shelves for CDs and games. Fit strip lighting under the shelving and an angle-poise light on the worktop. If the area looks business-like they will be more likely to get down to work. Set aside an amount in the budget for folders, boxes, files, notebooks and a new mouse mat for the computer.

You should also buy a comfortable, adjustable office chair to encourage good posture. Most furniture stores stock them and it is also worth having a look at second-hand office furniture shops because they deal with businesses that close down, so second-hand does not have to mean old and tatty.

Comfort zone

Once the work side of the room has been taken care of, you can turn your attention to the comfort zone. Seating can be soft and low with cushions and beanbags. If you have an old sofa to put in the room it can be covered with a fleece throw. Fleece comes in a wide range of colours and has the bonus of requiring no hemming and washing really well. Fake fur fabrics also make great throws, and are not expensive to buy by the metre. A decorator's cotton dustsheet covers most sofas, and can be machine dyed to the colour of your teenager's choice.

Coffee table

A low coffee table can be made from recycled wooden pallets. This wood is rough but soft, and is easy to smooth with an electric sander. The table surface can be faced with a sheet of hardboard edged with domed upholstery tacks, and four large castors will give it a contemporary edge. Another option is to head down to the second-hand shops and find something to make-over.

Teenagers need storage space too, especially if their study is part of their bedroom. Make sure they have enough places to put everything so they have no excuse for not tidying up.

Window dressing

Blinds or shutters which block out the daylight are usually popular with this age group. A room should be as dark as a nightclub first thing in the morning. Roller blinds with blackout backing work best if they are fitted into the window frame recess.

Fridge

And to finish off, include a small fridge. It may seem like a luxury, but it makes sense if long hours are to be spent working and relaxing in the room. Look for a bedsit or caravan fridge that will not take up too much space, and give it a colour lift with car spray paints. It will be the height of cool!

PROJECTS

The four projects on the following pages combine a sense of work with relaxation, to make a teenager's study as appealing as possible. Make sure you work as a team from the start, so that personal touches can be added along the way.

PROJECT ONE

Worktop

The big advantage of making a desk is that it can be made to fit the person and their specific requirements. If the desk is to be used for, say, a sewing machine as well as a computer, the sockets should be sited in a convenient position for both uses with all electrical cables channelled behind the unit. When you plan a unit to your own specifications, it can be easily fitted under a sloping ceiling or in an alcove. This plan is for building a worktop into a corner; the right type of shelves can be attached to the wall above it.

A worktop made specially for teenagers can be painted in their favourite colours, making work seem less of a chore.

HOW TO DO IT

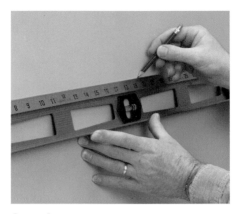

STEP 1 Decide upon the length and depth of the worktop, and then cut the timber to fit. Mark the position and height of the table on the wall. Use a spirit level to check the level.

STEP 2 Drill clearance holes through the battens approximately 25 cm apart, and then hold them up to the wall and mark their positions in pencil. Drill and plug the holes in the wall, and then screw the battens in place.

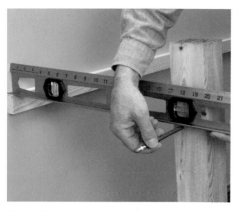

STEP 3 Cut the leg to the correct height. You will need an extra pair of hands to support it while you rest the batten on top; check that it is level before screwing it to the wall batten. Now add the final batten which completes the frame for the worktop. Check that it is level before screwing it to the leg and the wall batten.

STEP 4 Cut the sheet of MDF to fit the top exactly, and then cut out a channel at the back of the worktop to take all the electrical cables down to the socket. Sand smooth.

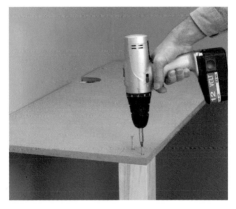

STEP 5 Drill clearance holes then screw the top to the battens and the legs.

STEP 6 Measure two fascia strips to fit on to the front and side of the worktop. Mitring the ends where they meet will give a more professional finish. Apply wood glue, and then secure the strips with pins using the small hammer. Sand, prime and paint the legs and fascia strips. The worktop can be protected with two coats of varnish, or a coat of paint. If you varnish the top then run a line of masking tape along its edge when you paint the fascia to guarantee a really straight line.

PROJECT TWO

Pegboard or softboard wall covering

Pegboard is perforated hardboard which can be used to cover sections or complete walls. It not only looks good, retro and funky but provides a really useful storage surface. The holes are used for hooks and pegs for hanging containers, small boxes, speakers and other gizmos. An alternative, useful and inexpensive material is softboard, which is usually used as a liner for school corridor walls. It is very lightweight, and can be stuck onto the wall with panel adhesive and then painted for use as a notice board.

Softboard makes an ideal noticeboard because it is lightweight, so it can be stuck on the wall with panel adhesive and painted a favourite colour. A few pop-star pin-ups and other teenage collectables will do the rest.

HOW TO DO IT

STEP 1 Hold the softboard against the wall and mark the position of the corners. Apply panel adhesive to the back of the softboard and stick it onto the wall.

STEP 2 Hold the moulding up to the wall and mark the position of the mitres. Drill clearance holes in three places along the length of each side. Mark the screw positions on the walls, and then drill and plug. Apply panel adhesive to the back of the mouldings and screw them to the wall.

STEP 3 Paint the softboard to blend in or contrast with the wall colour. Two coats may be necessary because it is highly absorbent.

YOU WILL NEED:

- HUBCAP
- DRILL
- CLOCK MOVEMENT
  AND HANDS
- BATTERY
- WIRE WOOL
- DETERGENT
- STICKY DOTS

PROJECT THREE

A hubcap clock

Making clocks is incredibly easy, costs very little and you can use any image you like for the face, including a photograph of someone or a hubcap! For a graphic effect apply brightly coloured sticky dots to the clock face instead of numerals. You will also need a battery-powered movement and a pair of hands, which come in a range of styles.

It is easier than you might think to make a clock, and you can make one out of almost anything. All you need is a clock movement with hands and your choice of 'clock face' (in this case, a hubcap) and you're there!

HOW TO DO IT

STEP 1 Clean off any dirt using wire wool and detergent.

STEP 2 Drill a hole in the centre of the hubcap for the clock movement.

STEP 3 Add the sticky dots to mark the hours.

STEP 4 Place the mechanism in the back and add the clock hands.

YOU WILL NEED:

• 75 CM EACH OF
ORANGE AND BLACK
(OR ANY COLOURS) OF
FLEECE FABRIC

• THREAD

• SEWING MACHINE

• NEEDLE FOR HAND
STITCHING

• BAG OF FOAM
CHIPPINGS OR
TWO PILLOWS
PER CUSHION

PROJECT FOUR

Floor cushions

If you have a sewing machine and can sew in a straight line there is no reason to buy large, expensive cushions. The best fabric for this sort of thing is fleece. It is inexpensive, comes in a wide range of funky colours and is something of a miracle because it is made from recycled plastic bottles! Buy 75 cm lengths of two different colours and then cut the two lengths in half. This will make two 75-cm-square cushions, and you can use both colours on each cushion.

Fleece cushion covers are perfect for lounging on a study floor after a hard few hours' studying. Fleece is a cheap fabric that comes in a huge range of funky colours.

HOW TO DO IT

STEP 1 Place one dark and one light square together with fluffy sides facing. Sew a line of stitches about 25 mm inside the outer edge, but leave a 20-cm gap for stuffing. Do the same with both cushions.

STEP 2 Fill the cushions with foam chips or a pair of pillows, and then use small slip stitches to close the gaps. Could anything be simpler?

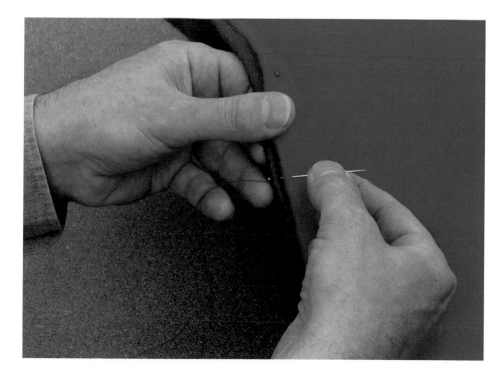

Child's playroom

If you have space for a playroom in your home then everyone is a winner. The children will love having their own activity room, and you will be able to gear their bedrooms towards relaxation and sleep, avoiding reminders of daytime excitement. A playroom is not just for kids though, it is somewhere for parents to relax with their children and friends without worrying about dangers or mess. The trick is to design a playroom that is virtually indestructible and danger free, without making it look like a padded cell!

To do this you design with children in mind, excluding things like slippery floors, sharp corners, tall but not out of reach shelving, trailing electric cables and doors that can slam on small fingers. It is not that you want a child who is unaware of danger and is incapable of recognising it but more that the playroom should be a sanctuary from it. Somewhere to let off steam. A place to be happy and uninhibited. Top 10 things to have in a great playroom might be…

A children's playroom is a perfect excuse for letting your imagination run wild. This playroom has been transformed into an exciting cowboys and Indians setting, complete with its very own jailhouse.

Vinyl flooring

A cushioned vinyl floor with a good quality underlay and a non-slip surface is the best flooring for a playroom. It has all the necessary qualities. Kids can safely scoot around, rollerskate, play with cars, fall on their knees and spill their drinks, while you have an easy-clean surface.

Bean bags

The original beanbag has been downsized for kids, and the same idea has been taken a stage further to make little armchairs with beanbag filling. Kids love sitting or lolling about in beanbags, and there are no hard edges to bump themselves on. As a security measure, stitch the metal end of the zip flat onto the fabric cover to prevent the ultimate snowstorm when the little darlings discover how to fling out the polystyrene beads!

Sofa

The comfortable sofa is for the adults. This is where you sit with your friends, or with a child on your knee watching a video or telling a story. An inexpensive sofa with a removable, washable cover in a bright colour is the ideal choice.

TV and video

A television in a playroom may seem something of a contradiction, but television is definitely part of a young child's experience. If the television is

surrounded by more hands-on, tempting things to do then it will not always win the battle for the child's attention. Sometimes children are soothed by the repetition of their favourite story or cartoon video, or want to watch them with their friends. The television can always be kept behind doors if you prefer not have it on show all the time.

Worktop for painting and drawing

Children love to paint and draw and they need access to paper, paints and crayons. They learn the rudiments at playschool, and will delight in endlessly painting their favourite subjects. You will need one or two low tables and chairs, an easel, paint pots, large brushes, anti-spill beakers for water and paints, wax crayons, aprons and a washing line with pegs to hang up the pictures to dry. Coloured paper, glue and safe scissors are the other must-haves.

Construction area

Children play with all kinds of building sets, beginning with basic wooden blocks before moving on to wooden trains, snap-together plastic bricks and miniature models of everything from galleons to spacecraft. The most important thing to know about construction toys is that each type must be kept separate otherwise they are never played with. This inevitably means a lot of hard sorting for parents, but make life easier by having an efficient storage system. Transparent plastic crates on castors are the perfect solution.

Blinds or curtains

The playroom will mostly be used in the daytime, but it is still nice to have the option of cutting out the daylight by pulling down the blinds or drawing the curtains. They are particularly useful for afternoon naps on the settee, a game of hide

Each set of games and construction toys needs to be kept separate or they will never be played with.

If you don't have space for a separate playroom, here's an idea for creating a separate one inside a bedroom – is it a greenhouse or is it a wendyhouse?

(Far right) A clever use of mural paint can create 3-dimensional mini-dramas on playroom walls.

and seek, shutting out the rain or reducing dazzling sunshine. And winter evenings always seem more cosy with the curtains drawn.

Sink

If there is a water source nearby have the pipes diverted and install a sink in the playroom. You will not regret it. It means that children can be cleaned up after painting, eating or accidents without leaving the room. The paint pots and brushes can be washed, cloths can be wrung out under the tap, and all this without leaving the playroom. A low square sink is ideal, but do have a thermostat on the hot tap to prevent scalds. Another good idea is to keep the plug on a high shelf to avert any catastrophic floods!

Easy-reach storage

One way to make short work of tidying up is to build a boxed seat along one wall with doors hinged along their top edge instead of on the side. They can then be lifted up like garage doors for putting boxes away. Another storage idea is to have a rail with pegs for hanging bags – plastic mesh satsuma bags are good because the contents are visible. Buy the storage crates first and build the shelves to fit them. It is also essential to have out-of-reach storage for art materials, a first-aid kit, face paints, board games and jigsaw puzzles – everything which you have out.

Bright lights

There is a difference between bright and harsh, and what you want is bright jolly lighting which makes it easy to find things, read books, paint pictures and play games. One or two 100 watt overhead pendant lights will illuminate the room, and a dimmer switch can be used to lower the light for quiet times. Angle-poise lights are useful for illuminating worktops, but use screw fittings to secure the lamp onto a shelf and avoid any type of lamp which could be knocked over.

When decorating the playroom include one area of wall painted with blackboard paint. This is guaranteed to be one of the most popular places in the room. Supply a large box of coloured chalks and a damp cloth to clean the board. Paint the other walls with bright cheerful colours and use as many special effects as you can find. Glitter glazes and scented paints are just two fun finishes that kids will love. And one of the following projects shows how to print a mural using foam blocks. It couldn't be easier or more effective. Deciding whether to allow children to help with the decorating is up to you – there are definite pros and cons (it can be difficult for a young child to understand why it's OK to paint on the walls in one room but not in another!) The floor project shows how to stencil a bold pattern of stripes, balls and stars on a painted wooden floor. This could also be done with vinyl floor paints to cheer up an existing vinyl floor. In a big room the floor can be treated like a playground and painted with a roadway, hopscotch, snakes and ladders or another favourite game. Let your imagination run wild and remember that the more fun you have while decorating, the better it will look.

YOU WILL NEED:

- OFF-CUTS OF
  UPHOLSTERY FOAM
- CRAFT KNIFE
- BIRO PEN OR FELT TIP
- SET SQUARE
- RULER
- A SELECTION OF
  EMULSION PAINT
  COLOURS
- PRE-MIXED
  WALLPAPER PASTE
  (DO THIS 5 MINUTES
  BEFORE YOU NEED IT)
- SEVERAL LARGE
  PLATES
- BRUSH FOR MIXING

PROJECT ONE

Mural printed with large foam blocks

Children have been building toy towns from shaped wooden blocks for a very long time, and this project does the same thing in two dimensions instead of three. Look out for a shop selling upholstery foam and buy off-cuts. They are easy to cut with a craft knife if you make the first cut along a drawn line, then bend the foam to open the cut and cut through the rest of it. Limit yourself to five bold shapes – a large square, a small square, an oblong, a triangle and an arch.

A colourful mural printed with foam blocks is far easier than a hand-drawn creation, but just as fun and inspirational.

HOW TO DO IT

STEP 1 Draw the pattern shapes onto card, using the set square and ruler to draw the geometric shapes accurately. Draw generously sized shapes in proportion to the wall width and height. Stick the shapes onto the foam.

STEP 2 Cut out the shapes. Make sure you have a sharp blade, and make the first cut in one go along the drawn line. The lower cuts to separate the foam pieces are not as important because they are not part of the printing surface.

STEP 3 Place a circle of each colour on a plate, and mix in the same amount of pre-mixed wallpaper paste. This will make the paint more gelatinous, and stop it from running if you have too much paint on the foam.

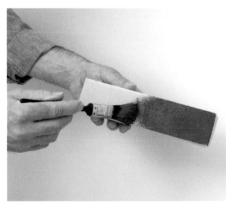

STEP 4 Dampen the foam, squeeze out any excess moisture and then begin to print. Press the block into the paint and test the print on a sheet of paper. Press the foam onto the wall to make a print. Build up the base blocks first.

STEP 5 Use the squares and oblongs to make a pair of pillars, and then print the arch shape over the top.

STEP 6 Top some of the squares with triangles, and keep on swapping the foam blocks and printing until the wall is covered with a toy town. A coat of clear varnish will help to protect and preserve the mural.

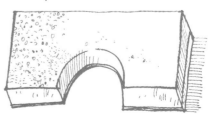

YOU WILL NEED:
- SHEET OF WAXED STENCIL CARD CUT INTO TWO 30-CM SQUARES
- CRAFT KNIFE
- PHOTOCOPY OF EACH PATTERN
- ADHESIVE SPRAY
- LARGE STENCIL BRUSH
- TWO WHITE PLATES
- ABSORBENT KITCHEN PAPER
- PAINT IN TWO CONTRASTING COLOURS (EITHER EMULSION AND VARNISH, OR A PREPARATORY FLOOR PAINT)
- CLEAR, STRONG POLYURETHANE VARNISH
- BRUSH TO APPLY THE VARNISH
- WHITE SPIRIT TO CLEAN THE BRUSH

PROJECT TWO
Stencilling a floor border

Stencilling on the floor is really easy, and you never get the problem of paint running as sometimes happens on walls. For this project you need a 30-cm square as the repeat, with two different shapes cut out of stencil card and alternated to form a border pattern around the edge of the room. This could be done on vinyl floor tiles with special vinyl paint, or using an emulsion paint with a varnish to seal it on wood. If you want a solid border then paint a 30-cm-wide background colour, or alternate two colours which can then be reversed for the pattern.

A stencil pattern border can brighten up either a wooden or a vinyl floor. For vinyl, use a special vinyl paint. Use a few repetitive patterns for a balanced, geometric effect.

HOW TO DO IT

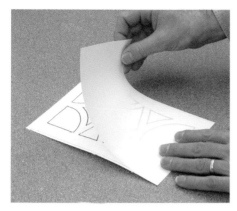

STEP 1 Photocopy the pattern so that it fills most of the stencil card – leave a 2–3-cm border around the edges so that the stencil is not too flimsy. Spray the back of the pattern with adhesive spray and stick it to the card.

STEP 2 Use a craft knife to cut out the stencils carefully. Always cut outwards from the corners, and try to cut curves with one even movement to avoid jagged edges.

STEP 3 Spray the back of the stencil with adhesive spray and leave for 5 minutes. Put a blob of each colour on the plates. You need a very small amount of paint for stencilling. Coat the brush with paint, and then dab most of it off on the kitchen paper.

STEP 4 Mark the guidelines in chalk if you are painting on to wooden floorboards, otherwise paint on to the coloured background. Place the stencil on the floor and smooth it flat. Apply the first colour.

STEP 5 Apply the second colour in exactly the same way.

STEP 6 If you are painting a wooden floor with emulsion apply 1–3 coats of varnish when the paint is bone dry. Floor paint is tough enough not to need varnish.

Use this guide to help you cut out the pattern for the stencil and position it on the correct place on your floor.

YOU WILL NEED:
- SHEET OF 12-MM MDF
- 2 LEGS FOR THE FRONT
  OF THE WORKTOP
  5 CM X 5 CM
- BATTENS FOR THE
  WALLS 5 CM X 2.5 CM
- 5-CM X 12-MM
  FASCIA MOULDING
  FOR THE TOP
- WOODFILLER
- No. 6 WALLPLUGS
- 25-MM PINS
- WOOD GLUE
- SANDPAPER
- PRIMER AND GLOSS
  OR MATT PAINT
- SPIRIT LEVEL IN A
  LONG RULE
- PENCIL FOR MARKING
- DRILL WITH A 6-MM
  MASONRY BIT
- PILOT, CLEARANCE
  AND COUNTERSINK
  BIT (USE A SCREWSINK
  FOR ALL THREE)
- BOX OF No. 6, 50-MM
  SCREWS
- HANDSAW
- SMALL HAMMER
- NAIL PUNCH
- PAINT BRUSH

PROJECT THREE

Making a low worktop

Children's furniture can be expensive to buy, so if you are fitting out a playroom it is well worth building a low, stable work surface. Begin by buying small chairs to match a low work surface, increasing the size of both as the children grow. Think about placing the work surface in a convenient place for electric sockets or wall lights, or in good natural light.

A low work surface is probably the most important item in a children's playroom. It is essential for painting, drawing, colouring-in and glueing, as well as other learning games.

HOW TO DO IT

STEP 1 Mark the height for the batten on the wall. Cut the batten to the correct length and drill clearance holes every 20 cm. Mark these as screw positions on the wall, and then drill and plug the holes.

STEP 2 Screw the batten to the wall. Rest the worktop on the batten and (with help) place the legs in position. Mark their cutting height having first checked the worktop with the spirit level.

STEP 3 Measure the fascia against the top and mark the position of the mitres

STEP 4 Glue and pin the fascia boards to the edge of the worktop.

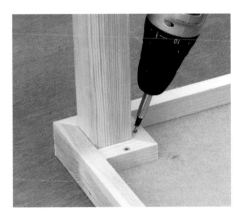

STEP 5 Mitre two battens to form a square collar to hold the leg firmly into the corner of the fascia. Screw into position.

STEP 6 Drill clearance holes and screw through the worktop to secure it to the wall-mounted batten.

YOU WILL NEED:

- SHEET OF SOFTBOARD (TIMBER MERCHANTS STOCK THIS)
- PANEL ADHESIVE
- HOCKEY STICK MOULDING TO SURROUND THE TOP AND SIDES
- No. 6 38-MM SCREWS OR 25-MM PINS
- WOOD FILLER
- 6-MM WALLPLUGS (IF USING SCREWS TO FIX)
- HANDSAW
- MITRING BLOCK
- DRILL WITH No. 6 MASONRY BIT, OR A SMALL HAMMER AND NAIL PUNCH
- CUPPED BRASS SCREWS

PROJECT FOUR

Fitting a pinboard above the worktop

It is a very good idea to fit a pinboard which runs the length of the worktop. This means that paintings and drawings can be pinned up to dry and be admired. A pinboard can be made from cork tiles or softboard which is inexpensive; it can be painted any colour to match the room.

Softboard makes an ideal pinboard because it is lightweight, so it can be stuck to the wall with panel adhesive and painted a favourite colour. Some paintings to be proud of will complete the look.

HOW TO DO IT

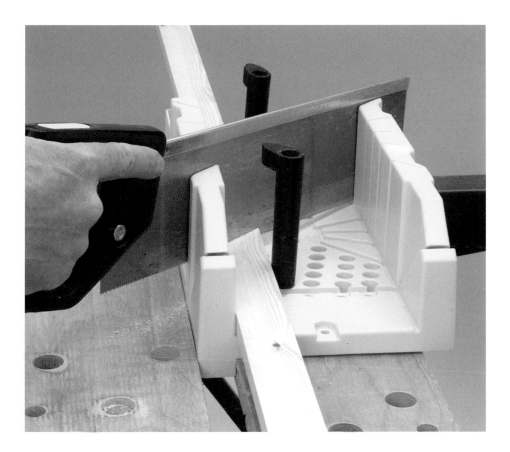

STEP 1 Measure and cut the softboard to fit. Cut the length of moulding for the top edge with mitred ends. Cut the two side pieces mitred to the top but straight at the bottom.

STEP 2 Fix the lower mitred moulding on to the wall first, using cupped brass screws.

STEP 3 Fix the rest of the frame to the wall. Apply a long squiggle of panel adhesive to the back of the softboard and attach to the wall.

Colour & light

Selecting colours can be completely daunting – there's such a huge range of choice it can be difficult to know where to start. But everyone's got their favourites and it's important to be surrounded by yours. But a combination of colour and light can also completely set the mood of a room, so it's useful to know about the qualities of different colours and the effects they can have. This section describes how colours can be used to create moods and different styles, and how a whole range of different lighting can enhance the function and atmosphere of a room.

Using colour to create moods

Colour can lift our moods, relax us, stimulate our senses and even make us feel uncomfortable in certain combinations. According to colour theory there are three primary colours – red, yellow and blue – from which all other colours are derived. To test this, put a blob of each primary colour on a white saucer and then mix equal amounts of two colours together. Red and yellow make orange, red and blue make purple, and yellow and blue make green.

Lilac is a calming colour because it is a product of blue, which is said to have a meditative effect. Be careful not to go too dark though – darker shades of lilac, which become violet purple, can be depressing.

These are the secondary colours, and by adding black or white you can darken or lighten them. By mixing combinations of different amounts of the primaries and black and white you can, in theory, make any imaginable colour. It is quite a science though, and beginners soon discover that most combinations soon turn grey or muddy brown! The paint companies have taken the guesswork out of colour mixing for us, and computers are used to dispense just the right amount of each component colour so that we can rely on colour number 3055b, for instance, to look the same every time.

Choosing colours

When choosing colours for a room, the first consideration should always be to choose a colour that you like, regardless of fashion. That is not to say don't experiment because otherwise you would probably never develop your own ideas. Try to raise your colour awareness by noticing combinations of colours that you like. And don't restrict yourself to just looking at colour in a decorating context because you may find the best inspiration elsewhere, for instance in a cookbook. A plate of salad, a bowl of fruit or heaps of vegetables on a market stall could equally provide the key to a brand new look for one of the rooms in your house. Holidays are also inspirational times because all our senses are more receptive to pleasure when we are relaxed and away from the pressures of everyday living. Take photographs of the landscape and buildings, the sea and any unusual colour combinations, and then see if you can pick out one colour scheme that reminds you of that time and place.

Making a complete colour change can be daunting, especially if your inspiration has come from a book or make-over television programme

where a room has been professionally styled with co-ordinating furniture and accessories. Strong colours invariably work well on television because the programmes need to make an impact in a short time, and there is not much room for subtlety. In your own home conditions are different, and you may find that the ideas which inspired you need to be toned down for everyday life. A strong colour is useful for defining the shape of a room and creating an atmosphere. It will set the mood for the whole home when used in the entrance hall, and it is a good way of defining your own space if you are sharing the living space with other people. Blue is a most versatile colour and was one of the last to appear in a full range of shades for home decorating because, until recently, the deepest shades were only available as pigments from art suppliers.

Red and yellow fabrics add warmth to a room with a wooden floor and create a modern country look.

This was also noticed with green because it derives from a mixture of blue and yellow. As the range of blues has expanded so have the greens. The most obvious newcomer that has become tremendously popular is lime green. It is sharp, sassy and youthful – the colour that nobody grew up with! Also note that in hot countries the light is much brighter, and strong colours work better than they do in the pale grey of Northern light. In fact colour cannot exist without light, and coloured light actually changes painted colour.

When darkness falls all colour disappears and red, blue and green become black – it's just a trick of the light!

Warming

If you have a cool room that needs warmth then use red, yellow and orange – the effect is immediate and warming. The intrinsic power of a colour is not lost in dilution either. A warm yellow could be a rich cream or an earthy ochre. These are the yellows which lean towards red and away from blue. In the same way choose reds which contain yellow rather than blue, like deep rusty brown, red ochre or deep burnt orange.

To keep a colour scheme warm avoid reds, purples or pinks that contain a lot of blue. These exotic colours like crimson, violet and cerise are good for highlights and flashes of brilliance, but they do not radiate warmth. A rosy pink with pea green and white is a natural combination that is fresh without feeling cool. Choose greens with a deep yellow cast like moss, pea and olive for warmth. Sage green is a neutral grey-green which can be warmed or cooled by the colours that surround it. Use it with deep reds and mustard yellow for a warm country look. Brown, rust and deep greens all look good with natural wood and fabrics, and the effect does not have to be old fashioned or heavy – mix woven fabrics like tweed with leather chairs, wooden flooring and rugs for a modern country look.

Cooling

In the Northern Hemisphere we tend to choose colours for warmth, but sometimes we need the opposite effect. If the coolness of a room is pleasant and desirable then enhance the effect with pale greens, icy blue or pale lemon yellow. Think of the Swedish look where the whites and greys of the landscape have been brought into

A cool room lacking in natural light can be brightened by white, and this is the perfect background for a crimson spotlight to add a splash of colour.

the home. The style is cool and minimal. In the Mediterranean countries houses are painted white to reflect the heat away from the house and keep it cool. Used indoors, white will brighten a cool room which lacks natural light without warming it, and help to create a tranquil atmosphere. All colours look good with white but the really strong contrasts look best in brilliant sunshine, as in the intense blues and whites of buildings on the Greek islands. A pale sky or lavender blue and white have an altogether more calming effect.

Red can add warmth to a room. Red and blue together, as two primary colours, make a strong contrast.

The colours of Africa have been brought into this room – the rusty red sofas complementing the wooden carvings and floor.

Citrus yellow with grey, black and white is sharp, cool and modern, and it looks especially good with the reflective metals like stainless steel, chrome or aluminium. Black and white are cool but hard, and being the ultimate contrast are best used where crisp lines are required on tiles or to make a traditional chequerboard floor.

Creating an atmosphere with colour

Certain styles and colour schemes are quickly recognisable, for example, New England, African, Caribbean, Far Eastern and so on. This makes it quite easy for us to recreate a particular atmosphere in our own homes, giving the living room the Moroccan look or a dining room a dash of Scandinavian, mostly with the use of colour. Different historical periods are also known for their colour schemes, which were sometimes more bizarre than you would imagine, and most paint companies produce historically correct colours for use in period homes. This does not mean living in museums and furnishing our homes with all the correct antiques. A Georgian or Victorian room returned to its original colours and furnished in a modern style can look elegant and seriously cool at the same time.

As a rule, light colour schemes will provide a lighter atmosphere, and so on. If you want your bedroom to look like a Turkish love nest begin by getting the colour right on the walls –

(Left) Pinks and purples in these silk and satin cushions suggest an exotic Turkish bazaar.

a deep Alizarin crimson is as passionate a colour as you can get and has its origins in the Ottoman Empire. Be inspired by colour combinations in paintings, carpets and textiles, and dress up the room with genuine oriental bazaar accessories like metal lanterns, scarves, beadwork and wall hangings.

Blues and yellows

Deep ultramarine blue is cool and atmospheric, and a room with walls painted this blue will appear bigger. The effect is the opposite to that of deep red, which can make the walls close in! Blue is said to be the perfect meditative colour, so choose this for a spiritual atmosphere. Yellow rooms are said to be stimulating to the senses and for this reason yellow is best avoided in bedrooms, especially of young children, where it might prevent a good night's sleep. Yellow is a good kitchen colour where its positive properties will give you the ideal start to the day. Lavender blue is the opposite – it is very calming but taken several shades darker to violet purple it can be depressing, so use purple sparingly unless it is contrasted with an equally powerful colour such as lime green, which will neutralise its depressive qualities. These two colours have become such an essential part of the modern decorator's palette that they will probably define our period as clearly as pale green, apricot and cream did in the early years of the 20th century.

(Above) The warm yellow of these walls is complemented by the Oriental purples of the lampshade, chair cover and floor cushions.

(Left) Green and white combinations have a fresh, cool effect. If you want a warmer green than the one shown here, choose one with a deep yellow cast, like moss, pea or olive green.

Using lighting effectively

The first thing to consider when decorating a room is the amount of natural light it gets and also when it gets the sun. This proportion of natural light and sunlight and the function of the room will help you make the correct lighting choices. Lighting should never be an afterthought in the decorating process and is something to consider from the start, especially if new sockets and channels for wall lights are needed. Remember this and you will never have the depressing task of channelling into a newly plastered and painted wall to fit a wall light!

It is not just colour that can affect mood – the way a room is lit can affect the whole atmosphere, so it is worth giving it as much consideration as you do the colour, furniture and accessories. Lighting has to be functional, but it is also aesthetic, so think about the function of the room as well as the mood you want to set for it. Good illumination can be created by using several different types of lighting, each of which has a different function.

Task lighting

When you are planning the lighting for your room first decide on which areas need strong light, or task lighting. These should be the work and reading areas, where it is essential for you to be able to see what you are doing. You will also need occasional strong lighting in some areas to illuminate cupboards, book shelves, hi-fi equipment or televisions, video recorders or writing desks.

(Right) Table lamps create pools of low light, which make a room more cosy and intimate.

(Far right) Inspection lamps, spotlights or just plain torches can be used to simulate lighting so you can buy a type suitable for a particular room.

Ambient lighting

Ambient lighting is another way of describing the light that is all around us. This background lighting simulates the natural daylight and takes the glare out of direct task lighting. Ambient light reveals the shape and size of the room and the colours used in it. A pendant fitting or a wall light fits this description.

Accent lighting

This type of lighting is either purely decorative, where the light itself is the decorative feature, or it is used to highlight and accentuate a piece of furniture or art in the room.

Buying lighting

Lighting is not an easy thing to buy because unlike other products, where you look before you buy, if you go to a crowded lighting showroom with no idea of what you are looking for, it will be practically impossible to judge the effect of an individual light when so many others are turned on. The best idea is to decide what kind of light you need and experiment in your home before you go out and buy it. Look in lighting catalogues for the different kinds of lights available, and magazines for how they look in situ. Then experiment by using torches, plug-in spotlights and inspection lamps to simulate wall washers, uplighters, downlighters, pendant lights, spotlights and table lamps. This is a job for two or more people, so invite friends round with their torches and turn a task into a party! There are lots of good lighting catalogues that supply goods by mail order, so there is no reason to feel limited to what is available locally. Most suppliers also understand the importance of seeing a lamp in your own room, and will be happy to exchange or refund when you return a light for purely aesthetic reasons.

Creating illusions

If you use a room during the day and it gets very little sunlight, you can make a room seem much sunnier by concealing white fluorescent tubes beneath pelmets above the windows. Daytime lighting is often necessary, especially in winter, but bulbs tend to create an unpleasant glare in natural daylight. Fit concealed halogen spotlights behind plants or furniture, and fluorescent striplights beneath wall cupboards to light worktops. Make any room appear more spacious by washing the walls with light from above or below. Disguise any features you dislike in a room by using angled spotlights to cast pools of light in another direction. A pendant light will appear to lower the ceiling height to where the light begins; use them in small rooms with high ceilings to change the proportions. A room will look more cosy and intimate with table lamps creating pools of low light.

Coloured lights

Tinted bulbs are useful for creating an atmosphere. Pale yellow will warm the room and pink will create a rosy glow. Stronger-coloured bulbs will knock out some of the colours completely – red or green cancel each other out, and blue will give a cool nightclub effect, which is perfect for summer parties. Red has the opposite effect, making a cool room seem instantly warmer. Christmas lights are also useful for adding instant sparkle, and use very little electricity. Put them around pictures, doorways or in glass fishbowls as feature lights with a party feel.

Candles

Candles give a room a unique atmosphere, and there has never been more choice than there is today. Gone are the days when a scented candle smelled like an air freshener – one candle can cost

Uplighters can make a ceiling look higher by casting it with light from below.

as much as a table lamp, but the scents on offer are so sublime that shops have trouble keeping up with the demand. The flicker of candlelight is the most romantic and relaxing type of light, and rows of nightlights bring a room to life.

Safety

There is one big downside to the candle boom and that is the rise in the number of house fires. Always use common sense when you site your candles, and never place them where there is the slightest chance of flames catching paper or fabric. It is also important not to leave candles burning unattended, but because while we all love to walk into a candlelit room, we can also ignore the safety advice. Very real danger comes from falling asleep or actually leaving the house with a candle burning: this should *never* be done.

(Far left) Halogen spotlights cast an ambient light which can be angled to cast pools in different directions.

Accessories

The finishing touches you add to a room are a chance to put a little of yourself into the style, whether it be in an arrangement of pictures, a choice of mirrors, a pile of cushions or a display of flowers. These final choices are fun to make, and usually take the least amount of time and effort. But they can also make or break the whole effect. This section gives a few things to think about when you're choosing these final touches.

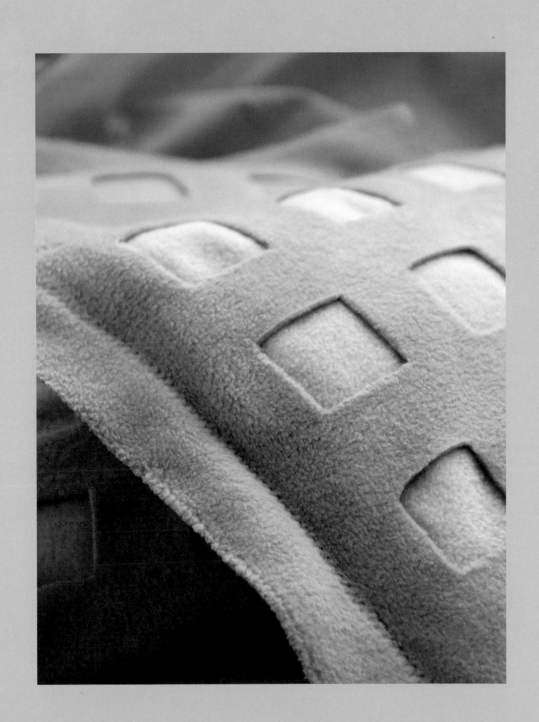

Accessories

The dictionary defines an accessory as 'a thing that is extra, useful or decorative but not essential'. These are the finishing touches to have some fun with when the paint has dried, the flooring is down and the curtains are up. This is where we allow our individuality to shine through, making our rooms reflect our lifestyles and personalities.

Walls without pictures or mirrors can make a room seem cold and unfriendly. Pictures are an ideal way of adding a splash of individuality to your walls.

Magazines and mail-order catalogues all use stylists, who are to rooms what hair and make-up people are to celebrities. The stylist's job involves keeping track of everything that already exists and is new to the accessory market, and their real skill is in knowing how to accessorise to best effect. Thanks to these tireless hunter-gatherers we get tons of visual reference and no shortage of shopping information. Treat yourself to a selection of different sources of inspiration – a good weekend colour supplement, a monthly homes magazine or a range of mail-order catalogues.

A room with individuality will often include a mixture of old and new objects or at least things sourced from different places: a set of matching cushions from a chain store, for instance, used next to an unusual lamp from a specialist lighting shop. Similar objects in varying styles will create areas of interest that will catch the eye. Black and white photographs arranged in a block of four matching frames on the wall will look smart and stylish, but a bit cold and contrived. Add one brightly coloured picture in an intricately carved wooden frame on a tabletop and the atmosphere will change immediately.

Not everything needs to be unique or expensive and it is worth perusing a few of the style magazine's 'best-buy' pages for recommendations. Keep a look out for the price comparison features, which show very similar designs with massive price differentials. You may fall in love with an impossibly expensive wrought-iron candelabra and be lucky enough to discover an almost identical version in a cheaper DIY outlet. Decorating has become very much like fashion and clothing in this way, with new styles sourced at the top end of the market then copied and quickly reproduced for mass consumption. Great news for the consumer, not so good for the designers under constant pressure to change styles and create new looks.

Frames and pictures

Walls without pictures or mirrors seem to absorb energy and interest from the room and, depending on their colour, can also make a room seem cold and unfriendly. There are so many framing options that it can be very confusing, and the right frame can make an ordinary image look impressive or quite the opposite. As a simple rule, most things look best with some white space around them, and a small image needs the most space between it and the frame. Sets of matching frames can look brilliant with very simple images of fruit or flowers, bold colourful art postcards or something more graphic, like letters of the alphabet or stamped numbers. The frames themselves can be the stars, especially if you trawl through antique and bric-à-brac markets. An ornate moulding can look fabulous around the most unlikely image. If you lack confidence, then buy framed prints from a good furniture and accessory store or a small gallery. The actual act of looking for something to put on your

walls will soon make you aware of what appeals to you and what doesn't. Ideally you should find something that will give you pleasure every time you look at it.

Cushions and throws

Gone are the days when a change of upholstery cost a small fortune, now all that's needed on an elderly sofa or chair is a new throw and a couple of cushions. Throws do a lot more than just disguising marks on the upholstery though, they are also useful for introducing a strong colour contrast, a more casual, relaxed style and a real sense of comfort. A throw can be the same colour as the sofa but a very different texture, for instance, mohair on linen or velvet on leather. Cushions and throws can be co-ordinated in fabric, texture or colour but beware of too many matching accessories – they can make a home look like a hotel. If you are short of money but want a new look buy a large cotton decorator's dustsheet and a packet of machine dye to make a giant throw to cover an old sofa. Spend any money left over on lovely cushions, or buy cushion pads and make the covers yourself. For colour and sparkle

at a reasonable price buy Indian or Chinese fabric; for florals buy an old chintz curtain and add a nice trimming; for knitted woollens or plain cottons adapt old shirts and jumpers by cutting off the arms and sewing up the top and bottom seams – the buttons stay put.

Vases, flowers and plants

If you allow yourself just one treat for the house once a week, make it a vase of fresh flowers. Even a bunch of wild flowers in a milk bottle on a wooden fruit box will make a house look like a home. Vases can be square, round, tall or short, and be made of glass or ceramic. They can even be left empty and still look good on a shelf. This is a way to add accent colour that can be changed to suit your mood. If fresh flowers don't match your busy lifestyle, then get a plant or two. Very beautiful house plants are often low maintenance in the right position, which is usually near light and out of draughts. Larger, more architectural plants, like palm, bamboo, cacti and the good old money plant, look good in contemporary surroundings. If you prefer something smaller with flowers, then orchids are the current must-haves.

Throws are an effective way of introducing a strong colour contrast, a more relaxed style and a sense of comfort.

Mini projects

Starting big decorating projects can be daunting so it's best to begin by tackling something small and satisfying so you can get your creative steam up and find that one thing leads to another. These projects will not take very long to complete and don't cost very much, but have been designed to give maximum satisfaction with minimum effort. A room can be perked up with new cushions, frames and lampshades, and sometimes all that is needed is a make-over for your existing accessories.

YOU WILL NEED:
• **A SELECTION OF BUTTONS**
• **TUBE OF CLEAR GLUE**
• **LAMPSHADE**

MINI PROJECT ONE

Lampshades

It is often difficult to find a lampshade to match the colour scheme of your room but there is no need to worry because lampshades can be painted with ordinary emulsion paint, and a sample pot of colour will be enough to transform two medium-sized shades or one large one. Plain colours look great, but patterns can be stamped or stencilled on, and you can also add trimmings such as a fringe, baubles or beads in contrasting or harmonising colours. The lampshade in the project is embellished with buttons stuck on with clear glue. Before the throwaway culture took over, every home had a button tin and these often turn up at flea markets and charity shops. Old buttons can be really beautiful and even the plain shell or mother-of-pearl types are well worth showing off on a lampshade or cushion cover.

Bases of lamps can be decorated as well as the shades. This seaside-style lamp base has been given a wet sand effect with shells attached using strong glue.

HOW TO DO IT

STEP 1 Plan the arrangement of the buttons on the shade. Apply a blob of glue to each.

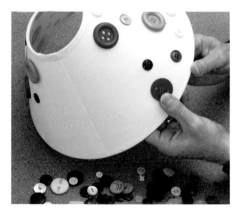

STEP 2 Hold it firmly against the shade until you feel the glue bonding. Continue with this until you have used all your chosen buttons.

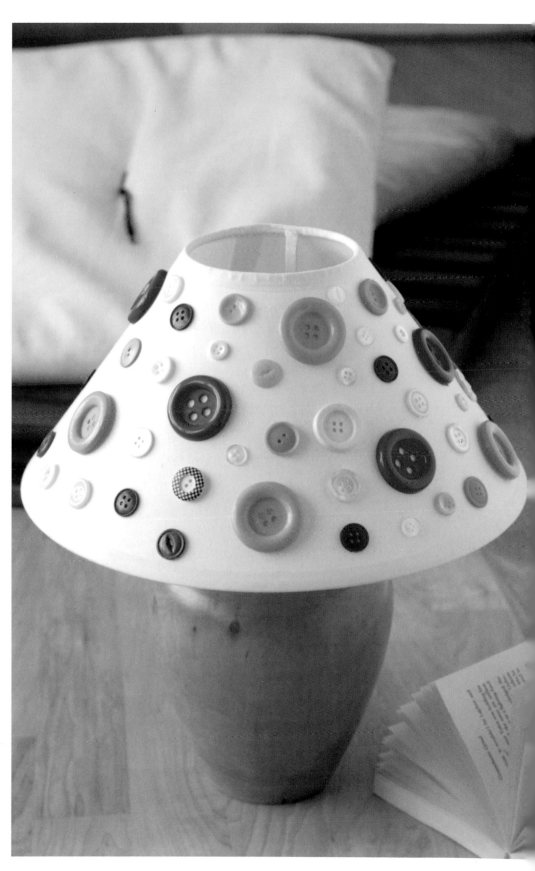

YOU WILL NEED:
- 50 CM FLEECE FABRIC IN COLOUR A
- 50 CM OF COLOUR B FABRIC WHICH IS HALF THE WIDTH OF COLOUR A
- STRAIGHT EDGE
- SCALPEL
- SEWING MACHINE
- SCISSORS
- THREAD
- PINS
- CARDBOARD TEMPLATE FOR CUT-OUT
- PEN

MINI PROJECT TWO

Cushions

There is no need to put up with grubby or faded cushions when a new set of covers is all you need to inject a bit of fresh style into the room. If your cushions feel lumpy, be bold and throw them away then treat yourself to some new ones. Cushion pads are not expensive and fabric can be bought either in remnant lengths or by the half metre. Check out charity shops and markets for lengths of fabric or clothing that can be cut down to make cushion covers. Shirts and cardigans make great covers as they already have a buttoned opening and you simply have to sew across under the arms and then cut off the top and the bottom. Evening dresses can be transformed into wonderfully exotic cushion covers for the boudoir, and an odd velvet curtain could be used to make a whole new set of cushions. There is also a lot of fun to be had with dyes and trimmings. If the bug really bites you, you could end up selling designer cushions from a stall of your own!

This stylish cushion cover can be made from fleece or felt, both of which do not fray when cut, so they will need no hemming. Fleece has the advantage of being washable so is the best choice if you want the cushions to last a while, and if you use a washable pad then the cushion can go in the washing machine and tumble drier.

A two-coloured cushion cover made out of fleece fabric is easy to make, and if used with a washable cushion pad, it can be put in the washing machine and drier.

HOW TO DO IT

STEP 1 Cut out three squares of fabric in the same size – two in colour A and one in colour B.

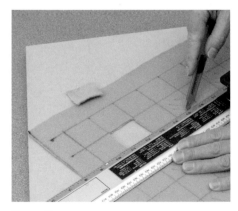

STEP 2 Mark the cut-outs by drawing around the template on the back of the colour B square. Use the scalpel and straight edge to cut out the shapes.

STEP 3 Place the colour B square on top of the other two and sew a line of close zigzag stitches to join the three layers on three sides. Put the cushion pad inside then sew up the fourth side.

YOU WILL NEED:
- FOIL WRAPPERS FROM TOFFEES AND CHOCOLATES
- PVA GLUE
- A SIMPLE FRAME
- SCISSORS OR A CRAFT KNIFE

MINI PROJECT THREE

Frames

Framed pictures on the walls make a house look like home, and there is no need to have bare walls just because you think you don't have any art worth framing. Make the frames into a focal point and pop anything inside them that fits in with the shape and colour scheme. You will be surprised how effective this can look. If your frame is square then pay a visit to a card shop and check out all the square cards. Once everyday objects are framed they assume a new importance, and can even become art! Try framing groups of bottle caps, buttons, labels or some unusual foreign packaging – most of these things have been designed by experts, so why not put them on show? When it comes to the actual frames, these can be picked up second hand for next to nothing at boot fairs or from market stalls. New frames from bargain stores can also be used, and sometimes all that is needed is a coat of paint to give them a new lease of life. Buy matching sets and paint them different colours, or buy lots of different frames and make them into a set by painting them a matching colour. There are so many ways in which they can be improved – it's just up to you to do it.

This wooden frame was about as plain and cheap as anything new can be, but now looks a million dollars with its shiny jewel-coloured covering. The metallic papers are sweet wrappers (yes, you have to eat the sweets first!), which are carefully smoothed out and stuck onto the frame in a patchwork pattern using PVA glue. This project is pure pleasure, from start to finish.

Old picture frames or cheap, new ones can be given this sparkling, jewel effect using sweet wrappers and glue. Try framing everyday objects inside to create an original work of art!

HOW TO DO IT

STEP 1 Smooth out enough sweet wrappers to cover the frame. They will need to overlap each other, and look best in a random patchwork pattern. Lay them out to decide on the colour arrangement.

STEP 2 Apply a coat of PVA to the frame, and then leave it to become tacky. Apply a coat of PVA to the back of each wrapper.

STEP 3 Smooth each wrapper onto the frame. Take care not to rip the fragile foil as you flatten it around the shape of the frame.

STEP 4 Use a sponge to ease the foil papers onto the frame and then wipe away any excess glue.

Suppliers

KITCHENS

Arriflo
Tel: 01708 526361 for your nearest stockist
Good for a wide range of taps

Astacast Sinks
Tel: 01024 477466 for your nearest stockist
Good for contemporary sinks

Berwyn Slate Quarry
Tel: 01978 861897
For slate worktops

Blanco
Tel: 020 8450 9100
Suppliers of sinks, taps and waste disposal units

Brass and Traditional Sinks
email: sales@sinks.co.uk

Formica
Tel: 0191 2590 3000 for nearest stockist

Gec Anderson Ltd
email: gec@ndirect.co.uk
Suppliers of trendy sinks and worktops

Granitops
Tel: 01980 862253
Suppliers of granite and marble for use as kitchen tops

IKEA
Tel: 020 8208 5600 for enquiries
Website: www.ikea.com

Magnet
Tel: 0800 192 192 for your nearest showroom
For fitted kitchens

Perstorp Warerite
Tel: 01753 886557 for your nearest stockist
For decorative laminated worktops

Scotts of Stow
email: sales@scottsofstow.demon.co.uk
Excellent for freestanding kitchen furniture and storage units

Wickes
126–138 Station Road
Harrow
Middsex
HA1 2QB
Tel: 0870 608 9001
DIY and building supplies

KITCHEN APPLIANCES

AEG
Tel: 01753 872500 for your nearest stockist
For general kitchen appliances

AGA-RAYBURN
Tel: 0345 125207 for your nearest Aga stockist
Tel: 0345 626147 for your nearest Rayburn stockist

The American Appliance Centre
Tel: 020 8529 9665
For US kitchen and laundry appliances

Appliance Direct
020 7221 1144
A good selection of ex-display, graded white goods

The Appliance Warehouse
Tel: 0115 984 4357
Lots of cheap appliances

The Classic American Fridge Company
Tel: 01923 490303

Flavel-Leisure
Tel: 01926 427027 for your nearest stockist
Suppliers of large, range-style double ovens

SMEG UK
Tel: 01235 861090
email: customer.service@smeguk.com
Good selection of contemporary favourites

Stanley Cookers
Tel: 01978 664576 for your nearest stockist
Cast-iron ranges, also used as heating boilers

BATHROOMS

Aqualisa Products
Tel: 0191 560000
Top quality showers

Armitage Shanks
Website: www.armitage-shanks.co.uk
For good quality sinks, baths and toilets

Bathroom Discount Centre

Tel: 0171 381 4222

Designer bathrooms at big discounts

C.P. Hart

Website: www.cphart.co.uk

Bathroom fittings and fixtures

Matki

Tel: 01454 328811

Modern and traditional shower
enclosures

Mira Showers

Tel: 01242 221221

Electric power and mixer showers

**Tubby DIY Bath Resurfacing Kit
(Brandon Products)**

Tel: 01302 788138

Works wonders on old baths, sinks
and toilets and is not expensive so worth
a try!

HOME OFFICE

IKEA

Brent Park

255 North Circular Road

London

NW10

Tel: 020 8208 5600 for your nearest
branch

Chairs, desks, filing cabinets and shelving
in great Scandinavian designs at good
value prices

Home catalogue and Ikea business
catalogue available

John Lewis

Tel: 020 7629 7711 for your nearest branch

Computers, office equipment,
storage, desks – in fact everything!

Delivery nationwide

Muji

Catalogue.

Tel: 0800 028 6063 for nearest branch
and brochure

Cool Japanese design at reasonable
prices, including desks, stationery, chairs
and storage solutions

Office World

Tel: 0800 500024

Furniture and stationery catalogue and
mail order

Rymans

Tel: 020 8569 3000 for your nearest
branch and mail order

Stationery, accessories and office furniture

TILES

Arosa Architectural

email: arosagroup@aol.com

Stainless steel tiles

Fired Earth

email: enquiries@firedearth.com

Best catalogue and a wonderful range
of glazed and natural tiles

Just Tiles

Tel: 020 8907 3020

Discount floor and wall tiles

Mosaics Direct

Website: www.mosaics.co.uk

Original Style Tiles

Website: www.originalstyle.com

Victorian and other styles of tile

The Reject Tile Shop

Tel: 020 7483 2608

Quality seconds

Tiles Galore

Tel: 020 8677 6068

Tiles imported direct from foreign factories

WALL PANELLING

Craftmaster

Website: www.masonite.co.uk

Chair-height wall panelling

Market Square, Warminster

Tel: 01985 841041

Soft wood panelling

Norske Interiors

Tel: 01472 240832

Ready-painted tongue and groove
panelling

Oak Master

Tel: 0117 947 7878

For if you want traditional-looking
panelling

SOFT FURNISHINGS

Fabric World

Tel: 020 8688 6282

Designer curtain and upholstery fabric

Ian Mankin

Tel: 020 7220 997

Natural cottons, linens, tickings and
ginghams. Mail order only

John Lewis
Tel: 020 7629 7711 for your nearest branch
Website: www.johnlewis.com
Upholstery, curtains, blinds and cushions
Delivery nationwide

Just Fabrics
Website: www.justfabrics.co.uk
Own range, plus some designer
clearance stock

FLOORING

Amtico
Tel: 0247 686 1400 for brochure
Website: www.amtico.com
Vinyl flooring

carpet.uk.com
Web-based carpet store

Courts
Tel: 0800 731 2121 for your nearest
showroom
Good value wood-effect laminated
flooring (not for kitchen or bathroom use)

Crucial Trading
Tel: 0800 374429 for brochure
Natural floor-coverings in jute, sisal
and seagrass

e-RUGS
Website: www.e-rugs.co.uk
Rugs on-line

Hardstuff
Website: www.hardstuff.co.uk
For tough slate flooring

Harvey Maria
Tel: 020 8516 7788
Website: www.harveymaria.co.uk
Wacky floortiles for virtual
environments, including water, grass,
florals and many more

Pergo
Tel: 0800 374 771
Website: www.pergo.com
Laminate and floorboards. Brochures
on request

Roger Oates
Website: www.oates.demon.co.uk
Top-quality, natural materials for stair
carpets and runners

The Rug Company
email: rugcompany@compuserve.com
Durries and rugs

Slate World Ltd
www.slate-world.com

Terracotta Direct
Website: www.terracottadirect.com
Handmade tiles from Spain

Victorian Woodworks
Website: www.victorianwoodworks.co.uk
Handmade and recycled wooden flooring

Wicanders
Website: www.wicanders-amorim.co.uk
Cork flooring and linoleum

CRAFT MATERIALS

Hobbycraft
Website: www.hobbycraft.co.uk

Home Crafts Direct
Website: www. speccrafts.co.uk

PLASTER MOULDINGS

Stevensons of Norwich
Website: www.stevensons-of-
norwich.co.uk

WALL COVERINGS

Graham & Brown
Tel: 0800 328 8452
Website: www.grahambrown.com
New-style wall textures, with a good
metallic range

Stencil Library
Tel: 01661 844844
Big range of all styles of stencil.
Catalogue and mail order

BLINDS

Eclectics
email: info@eclectics.co.uk
Contemporary blinds

Hillary's Blinds
Website: www.hillarys.co.uk
Permanent bargains, includes measuring
and fitting service

PAINT

Zest
Tel: 020 7351 7674
Superior Mediterranean paints plus
a range of chalky-finish paints

Crown Paints

Tel: 01254 704951

Dulux

Tel: 01753 550 555 for your nearest stockist

Website: www.dulux.com

Farrow & Ball

Website: www.farrow-ball.co.uk ·

A large selection of historic colours based
on the National Trust houses

International Paints

Tel: 01962 717 001/002

Website: www.plascon.com

Specialist paints for vinyl, melamine,
floors, radiators, concrete and much more

Paint Library

Tel: 020 7823 7755

Good quality paint and beautiful
colour ranges

Ray Munn

Tel: 020 7736 9876

Good specialist paints and primers

FURNITURE BLANKS

Scumble Goosie

Website: www.scumble-goosie.co.uk

Unpainted MDF and wooden furniture

MAIL ORDER FURNISHINGS

Bombay Duck

Website: www.bombayduck.co.uk

Trendy Eastern style

Habitat

www.habitat.co.uk

The Holding Company

Website: www.theholdingcompany.co.uk

Stylish storage specialists

Home Elements

www.homeelements.co.uk

Marks & Spencer

Website: www.marks-and-spencer.co.uk

McCord Design By Mail

www.mccord.uk.com

Next

Tel: 0345 100 500

Website: www.next.co.uk

Full interiors range

Ocean

Tel: 0870 242 6283

Website: www.oceancatalogue.com

Stylish contemporary mail-order company

DIY SUPERSTORES

B&Q

Website: www.b-and-
q.co.uk/www.diy.co.uk

Focus Do It All

Tel: 0800 436 436 for your nearest branch

Homebase

Tel: 0645 801 800 for your nearest branch

LIGHTING

BHS

Tel: 020 7262 3288 for your nearest branch
Excellent lighting range at very
reasonable prices

Christopher Wray Lighting

Tel: 020 8366 869

Website: www.christopher-wray.com

Big range of traditional and
contemporary styles. Catalogue and
mail order

Electrical Contractors Association

Tel: 020 7313 4800

Website: www.eca.co.uk

List of approved electricians

Great Mills

Tel: 0800 052 4404

Website: www.greatmills.co.uk

Good range of lighting and other
furnishings

Osram

Website: www.osram.co.uk

For every sort of bulb

Index

A

accent lighting 233

accessories 93, 101, 236–9

African sitting rooms 64–5

aluminium 30–1, 72–3

ambient lighting 233

appliances 18, 26, 248

armchairs 45

atmosphere 230–1

B

bathrooms

    contemporary 168–75

    shower rooms 176–83

    suppliers 248–9

    traditional 156–67

bean bags 212

bedrooms

    children 132–9, 140–5

    contemporary 108–15

    fantasy 140–5

    teenage boys 116–21

    teenage girls 122–31

    traditional 100–7

beds 104–5, 108–9

    drop-in surrounds 112–13

    fantasy bedrooms 140, 142–5

    scaffold pole bedheads 118–19

blackboard paint 138, 214

blinds

    children's bedrooms 132

    contemporary bedrooms 110

    contemporary kitchens 19

    contemporary sitting rooms 55

    nurseries 146–7

    office areas 186, 187, 195

    playrooms 213–14

    studies 203

    suppliers 250

    teenagers' bedrooms 123

blocking 96–7

books 133

breakfast bars 32–3, 36–7

C

caddies 182–3

candles 56, 235

carpenters 169, 176

carpets 45

castle theme 140–5

CDs 57, 187, 202

ceramics 27

chairs

    bedrooms 128–31

    dining rooms 78, 82–5, 87

    kitchens 19, 27, 35

    nurseries 147

    office areas 187, 193–4

    sitting rooms 45, 56

changing tables 147, 150–1

chequered borders 26

children 176, 192, 202

    bedrooms 132–9, 140–5

    dining rooms 87

    playrooms 212–23

choosing colours 227–8

chrome 19, 22–3, 26

clocks 208–9

coffee tables 55, 60–1, 203

colours

    bathrooms 169

    bedrooms 110, 116, 123, 132

dining rooms 79, 87, 92, 96–7

grouting 172–3

kitchens 10, 18–19, 26, 35

lighting 235

nurseries 146

selecting 224–31

sitting rooms 62

comfort zones 114–15, 203

computers 52, 120–1, 186–7, 202

concealed uplighters 88–9

construction areas 213

contemporary styles

    bathrooms 168–75

    bedrooms 108–15

    dining rooms 86–91

    kitchens 18–25

    sitting rooms 54–61

cool colours 228–9, 231

cots 147

counters 35

country kitchens 10–17

craft materials 250

crib 147

cubed units 186

cupboards 12–15, 101, 186

curtains

    bathrooms 162–3

    bedrooms 110, 124–5, 141

    dining rooms 94–5

    nurseries 146

    playrooms 213–14

    shower rooms 180–1

    sitting rooms 45, 50–1, 55

curved desks 200–1

cushions 239, 244–5

    children's bedrooms 139

contemporary sitting rooms 56

teenagers' rooms 126–7, 210–11

traditional sitting rooms 45, 48–9

D

decluttering 57, 101, 111

denim tab-top curtains 124–5

desks

office areas 186–91, 200–1

teenagers' rooms 120–1, 204–5

dining rooms

contemporary 86–91

sitting/dining 92–7

traditional 78–85

displays 10–11

distressed paintwork 11

dividers 94–5, 186

DIY superstores 251

doors

contemporary kitchens 20–1

country kitchens 12–15

galley kitchens 34

tiny sitting rooms 70–1

drawers 57

dressing tables 106–7, 122

E

easy-reach storage 214

eco-friendly materials 54–5

electricians 168, 176, 202

electricity 157, 193, 202

ensuite shower rooms 177

etching spray 166–7, 169, 174–5

F

fabrics 55

filing 187

fireplaces 44

fitted carpets 45

fixtures and fittings 156–7, 168, 176, 193–4

floating shelves 40–1

floating wooden floors 54, 58–9

floor cushions 210–11

floors

bathrooms 158, 164–5, 169, 171

bedrooms 101, 111

dining rooms 86, 92

kitchens 18, 26, 34

office areas 195

playrooms 212, 218–19

shower rooms 178–9

sitting rooms 54, 58–9

studies 202

suppliers 250

flowers 239

foil squares 72–3

fold-away counters 35

formica 27

four poster beds 104–5

frames 45–6, 238–9, 246–7

fridges 203

frosted glass shelves 18

furniture

blanks 251

children's bedrooms 138

contemporary bedrooms 108–10

office areas 186–7, 193–4

sitting/dining rooms 93

suppliers 251

teenagers' bedrooms 116–17

G

galley kitchens 34–41

gingham walls 148–9

glass shelves 34, 54

glass table tops 86

global sitting rooms 62–9

grouting 172–3

H

halogen spotlights 19, 235

handles 24–5

hinged breakfast bars 36–7

homework 117

hubcap clocks 208–9

K

kitchens

1950s 26–33

contemporary 18–25

country 10–17

galley 34–41

suppliers 248

kitsch 27

L

lamps 56, 123, 235, 242–3

leather cubes 56

lighting

bathrooms 157–8, 168

bedrooms 101, 110, 123, 132–3

dining rooms 87, 88–9, 92

kitchens 10, 19, 35

nurseries 147

office areas 187, 196–7

playrooms 214

selecting 224, 232–5

sitting rooms 46

suppliers 251

M

magazines 57

mail-order furniture 251

Mediterranean sitting room 68–9

mobiles 152–3

moods 226–31

Moroccan sitting room 66–7

mosaics 177

murals 216–17

N

nurseries 146–53

O

office areas 186–201, 249

P

packaging 27

paintings 45–6

paintwork

    contemporary bathrooms 169–71

    distressed 11

    floorboards 164–5

    suppliers 250–1

panelling 134–5, 160–1, 249

patterns 27, 166–7

peg rails 136–7

pegboards 206–7

photocopied fun cushions 139

photographs 45–6, 133

pictures 238–9

pinboards 222–3

pine duckboards 178–9

pink pony chairs 128–31

planning

    contemporary bathrooms 168–9

    offices 192–5

    teenagers' studies 202–3

    traditional bathrooms 156

plants 239

plaster mouldings 250

plastics 27

play areas 132

playrooms 212–23

plumbers 168, 176, 177

polka dots 27

posture 193

power showers 177

prints 45–6

R

rails

    bathrooms 168

    bedrooms 109, 122, 136–7

    kitchens 19, 22–3, 40–1

    shower rooms 176

recessed downlights 19

repetitive strain injury (RSI) 187

room dividers 94–5, 186

rosewood graining 90–1

rugs 45, 55

S

safety 235

sanitaryware 168–9

scaffold pole bedheads 118–19

screens 52–3, 92, 186

second-hand furniture 86, 193–4

Shakers 109

shelves

    bathrooms 168, 169

    bedrooms 136–7, 141

    frosted glass 18

    galley kitchens 34, 40–1

    office areas 187

    sitting rooms 46, 54, 57

short rooms 71

shower rooms 176–83

showers 157, 176–83

sinks 214

sitting rooms

    contemporary 54–61

    global 62–9

    sitting/dining rooms 92–7

    tiny 70–5

    traditional 44–53

slatted blinds 19

sockets 193, 202, 204

sofas

    contemporary sitting rooms 56

    office areas 194

    playrooms 212

    traditional sitting rooms 46

soft furnishings 249–50

splashbacks, 1950s kitchens 30–1

spotlights 19, 235

stainless steel see steel

stars 27

steel

    appliances 18, 26

    contemporary dining rooms 86

    1950s kitchens 27, 30–1

stencilling 102–3, 218–19

stools

    contemporary kitchens 19

galley kitchens 35, 38–9

office areas 194

storage

children's bedrooms 133

contemporary bathrooms 168

contemporary sitting rooms 54, 57

galley kitchens 35, 38–9

office areas 198–9

playrooms 214

teenage girls' bedrooms 123

tiny sitting rooms 74–5

traditional bathrooms 159

traditional bedrooms 100

stripes 80–1

studies 202–11

stylists 238

suppliers 248–51

T

tables

changing 147, 150–1

contemporary kitchens 19

contemporary sitting rooms 55, 60–1

rosewood graining 90–1

teenage girls' bedrooms 122

teenagers' studies 203

traditional bedrooms 106–7

traditional dining rooms 78–9

tall rooms 71

task lighting 35, 232

teenagers

boys' bedrooms 116–21

girls' bedrooms 122–31

studies 202–11

televisions 52, 212–13

textures 114–15

throws 45, 47, 56, 239

tiles

contemporary bathrooms 169, 170

country kitchens 16–17

floors 26

suppliers 249

tiny sitting rooms 70–5

tongue-and-groove panelling 134–5, 160–1

toys 133, 141

traditional styles

bathrooms 156–67

bedrooms 100–7

dining rooms 78–85

sitting rooms 44–53

U

units

contemporary kitchens 18

contemporary sitting rooms 57

cubed 186

1950s kitchens 28–9

office areas 186–7, 188–91

teenagers' studies 202–3

upgrades 169

uplighters 88–9

utensil rails 19, 22–3

V

vases 239

video games 202

video recorders 52, 212–13

video tapes 57

vinyl floors 171, 212

W

walls

children's bedrooms 134–5

coverings 250

nurseries 148–9

office areas 194–5

teenagers' studies 206–7

traditional bathrooms 158, 160–1

traditional bedrooms 101, 102–3

warm colours 228, 231

willow baskets 14–15

windows

contemporary bathrooms 174–5

contemporary bedrooms 110

nurseries 146–7

office areas 195

teenagers' studies 203

tiny sitting rooms 70–1

traditional bathrooms 166–7

traditional bedrooms 101

wood

contemporary dining rooms 86

floors 54, 58–9

graining 90–1

kitchen units 18

storage cubes 54

worktops

contemporary kitchens 19

country kitchens 16–17

playrooms 213, 220–1

studies 204–5

Z

zinc 30–1

Acknowledgments

The authors would particularly like to thank Clare Shanahan,
for her irrepressible good humour, patience and expert
styling of the photographs.
They would also like to thank Alistair's mum Doris
for her patience during the photoshoot.

The publishers would like to thank the following for loan of props:
Embrotrap (Oriental) Market, 10 Church Road, Hove, East Sussex;
Evolution, 42 Bond Street, Brighton, East Sussex;
Interior Illusions, 46 High Street, Old Town, Hastings;
Middle Farm, Firle, East Sussex;
Saffron, 21 Bond Street, Brighton, East Sussex;
The Ship Wreck Centre, Rock-an-ore, Hastings, East Sussex;
Stewart Gallery, 48 Devonshire Road, Bexhill, East Sussex;
Sussex Marble, 16 Wainwright Close, St. Leonards on Sea, East Sussex;
T.C. Carpets and Beds, Earl Street, Hastings, East Sussex;
W.H.Clarke Scaffolding, Hackney Road, London;
Wood Bros, 66 George Street, Brighton, East Sussex.

The publishers would also like to thank the following for use of copyright material:
ELIZABETH WHITING & ASSOCIATES: pp. 10, 11, 18, 19, 26, 27, 34, 35, 44, 45, 46, 54, 55, 56, 57, 62, 63, 71, 78, 79,
86, 87, 92, 93, 100, 101, 108, 109, 110, 111, 116, 117, 122, 123, 132, 133, 140, 141, 146, 147, 156, 157, 158, 159, 168, 169,
176, 177, 186, 187, 192, 193, 194, 195, 202, 203, 212, 213, 214, 215, 226, 227, 228, 229, 230, 231, 232, 233, 234, 235, 238, 239, 242.